George Coulson Workman

The Old Testament Vindicated as Christianity's Foundation Stone

George Coulson Workman

The Old Testament Vindicated as Christianity's Foundation Stone

ISBN/EAN: 9783337166144

Printed in Europe, USA, Canada, Australia, Japan

Cover: Foto ©Lupo / pixelio.de

More available books at **www.hansebooks.com**

THE
OLD TESTAMENT VINDICATED

AS

CHRISTIANITY'S FOUNDATION-STONE.

BY

GEORGE COULSON WORKMAN, M.A., Ph.D.,

Author of "The Text of Jeremiah," etc.

WITH

An Introduction

BY

NATHANAEL BURWASH, S.T.D., LL.D.,

Chancellor of Victoria University, Toronto.

TORONTO:
WILLIAM BRIGGS,
Wesley Buildings.

Montreal: C. W. COATES.   Halifax: S. F. HUESTIS.

1897.

CONTENTS.

	PAGE
PREFACE	5
INTRODUCTION	11

CHAPTER I.
ESSAY 17

CHAPTER II.
OCCASION 23

CHAPTER III.
METHOD 29

CHAPTER IV.
INSPIRATION 34

CHAPTER V.
REVELATION 40

CHAPTER VI.
EVOLUTION 46

CHAPTER VII.
INTERPRETATION 52

CHAPTER VIII.
CITATION 59

CHAPTER IX.
HISTORY 65

CONTENTS.

	PAGE
CHAPTER X.	
PATRIARCHS	73
CHAPTER XI.	
SCIENCE	79
CHAPTER XII.	
RELIGION	87
CHAPTER XIII.	
MORALITY	95
CHAPTER XIV.	
BARBARITY	101
CHAPTER XV.	
SACRIFICE	107
CHAPTER XVI.	
ELECTION	113
CHAPTER XVII.	
ANTHROPOMORPHISM	119
CHAPTER XVIII.	
MIRACLE	125
CHAPTER XIX.	
PROPHECY	131
CHAPTER XX.	
IMMORTALITY	137
CHAPTER XXI.	
QUALITIES	148

PREFACE.

A BRIEF synopsis of these pages appeared in the columns of the *North American Review* for May, 1896. The appreciative criticism of the press, as well as the special importance of the subject, has impelled me to prepare the present volume.

Though a comparatively small book, it is very compactly written, and contains a pretty large amount of matter. It treats in a concise way of the leading features of the Old Testament, and deals in a critical way with the chief objections that have so often been made in one form or another, by one prejudiced writer after another, against the Old Testament. So far as I know, it is the first attempt yet made to give a complete answer to such objections from the standpoint of modern Christian criticism.

Besides answering sceptical objections, I have shown the sense in which the Old Testament is an organic part of the New Testament. I have also shown the ethical and religious value of the ancient Scriptures in their inner spiritual relation to Christ and Christianity. On every point, too, I have aimed to be not simply defensive, but constructive.

In former times, religious scholars have so magnified the influence of God in the composition of the Scriptures as to see nothing but a divine element in the Bible; and, for a long time, rationalistic scholars have so exalted the reason of man in the evolution of religious ideas as to deny the presence in it of any element other than human. The one class was as uncritical as the other class is unevangelical.

At the present time, however, a Biblical interpreter is not compelled to be either uncritical or unevangelical. The alternative is no longer a choice between rationalism and traditionalism, but a choice between a rational and a mechanical view of Scripture. Christian scholars now acknowledge a twofold element in the Bible;

but, while they perceive two elements in it, they hold as firmly to the divine element which faith recognizes as to the human element which reason sees.

With a full recognition of the divine element, I have indicated certain human characteristics of the ancient record, a knowledge of which is essential to its true interpretation. In other words, by an impartial consideration of the human element, which has special features as well as special prominence in the Old Testament, I have pointed out the way in which every fundamental difficulty may be fairly and reasonably explained.

When answering objections or expounding passages, it is scarcely necessary to say, I have conceded nothing and concealed nothing. No concession of truth is required to defend the Scriptures from misrepresentation; and no concealment of fact respecting the Scriptures can permanently help the cause of Christianity. I have tried, indeed, to let the Old Testament vindicate itself. It does not need apology so much as explanation. To understand it is to prize it.

Some people foolishly suppose that criticism has undermined the authority of the Old Testament, but such is not by any means the case. Criticism has merely corrected wrong views of the Old Testament, and rectified mistaken notions as to its meaning and purpose. Criticism does not diminish, much less undermine, the true authority of any part of Scripture, for the simple reason that nothing can shake the authority of divine truth. Hence the proved results of criticism, like the proved results of science, are calculated not to unsettle, but to establish faith, not to disturb, but to promote peace, not to disquiet, but to produce rest.

It is a matter for regret that reverent criticism should ever have been regarded as inimical to religious belief. Instead of finding it hurtful to their religion, those who understand its aims and methods find it helpful to their religion. To multitudes of students it has already made the Bible practically a new book. What Christian criticism has done, Christian criticism will continue to do. It will make the precious old Bible a blessed new book—new in the interest it awakens, new in the meaning it yields, new in the beauty it reveals, new in the authority it imposes and enforces, namely, the authority of certified or established truth.

In consequence both of misconception and of misrepresentation, therefore, a popular work, setting forth in brief its character and qualities, seems to be specially needed for the use of those who have not the opportunity of studying it critically. A proper knowledge of the Bible is the best means of saving men from scepticism about the Bible.

This book has been written with the belief that all who read it will feel that there is nothing about the Old Testament that needs to be renounced but a traditional view of its origin and structure, and also that there is nothing about it that needs even to be modified but an erroneous theory of the inspiration of its authors and an irrational method of interpreting its books.

The volume is now published in the hope that those readers who, because of sceptical attacks on the Old Testament, have become indifferent or prejudiced in regard to it, will see that the only thing about it that ought to be discarded is an old-fashioned way of viewing and treating its literature.

G. C. WORKMAN.

Toronto, May, 1897.

INTRODUCTION.

THIS tersely written volume is the outcome of one of the most serious phases of our present day life. We are in the midst of a crisis of thought which two directly opposite classes of men regard as destructive of religious faith. The dogmatist, on the one hand, and the rationalist, on the other, both look upon the movement as subversive of the very foundations of Christianity. The former views the threatened result with dismay; the latter views it with indifference, if not with satisfaction.

As a matter of fact, however, neither true religion nor the spiritual power of Christianity has been seriously disturbed by the movement. In no other age of the world have there been so many living witnesses, both to the moral influence of the Gospel and to its blessedness as an inner spiritual force, as there are to-day. Even as it was after Pentecost, so it is now. The number of true believers is being continually multiplied, and millions of men are daily finding rest to their souls, as well as light upon the whole pathway of life, by drawing near to God their Father through Jesus Christ his Son.

How does it happen that these two apparently incompatible facts are both so specially prominent in our age? An answer is not difficult to give. In my opinion, it is this. The two facts represent two movements which are essentially distinct. The one is intellectual, the other is moral; the one touches our theology, the other touches our religion. Our theology, without doubt, is seriously disturbed; but our religious life is moving forward from year to year with increasing spiritual power and to richer practical results.

But this peculiar combination of circumstances is not a new thing in the Church's history. Christianity itself was a terrible subversion of the old Jewish theology; but it was life from the dead, so far as religion was concerned. The Reformation was an utter confusion of the mediæval dogmatism; but it brought a deeper, stronger, freer religious life. John Wesley practically discarded the rigid Calvinistic dogmatism of his day; but he made a more rational theology a mightier instrument for the extension of evangelical religion. In each of these instances, the revolt of reason from ancient dogmatic superstitions was accompanied with, or rather preceded by, a remarkable increase of new spiritual life.

During the present century, the intellectual and the spiritual movement have been too widely separated. Our great evangelists have not been our great thinkers, critics, or philosophers. We have lacked a Paul, a Calvin, a Wesley to reconstruct the intellectual form in which the new spiritual life might be expressed. The result has been an undue alarm, as well as a futile effort to rehabilitate the old formulæ, on the one hand, and an almost utter despair of Christianity, if not of religion itself, on the other hand, the cry in each case coming to us from earnest hearts that not only feel but think.

In recent years, God has been raising up a new class of men in whom, I believe, the hope of the future very largely lies. They are spiritual-minded men of profound faith in God, in Christ, and in the light of the Holy Spirit; and, therefore, they are men who can be trusted to hold fast the foundations of Christianity. But they are also men who recognize the true office and the indefeasible rights of reason in the search for truth, as well as in the construction of theology. Drummond, in the field of science; Driver, Dods and George Adam Smith, in the field of Biblical criticism; Fairbairn, in the field of systematic theology; and Bruce, in the field of apologetics, are examples of an influential and rapidly increasing body of scholars who are striving for the reconciliation of religious faith with rational criticism.

No one, of course, claims for any of these men infallibility, or even approximate perfection of results. As human beings, compassed with infirmity, they have all made mistakes. Having been pioneers in their respective departments, they have suffered the disadvantage of the prophets of all past ages, in that they have been suspected, and even rejected, by both classes of persons whom they have striven to help. The orthodox have been ready to call them disloyal; and those whose reason was beset with doubts and difficulties have feared that they were only men of compromise, who could not lead any one to a trustworthy basis of belief.

Notwithstanding the disadvantage they suffer, however, such scholars are right. They desire honestly to make use of every means of arriving at truth which the Divine Being has provided for us. In using the means thus provided, they hold as loyally to the inner faith of our moral and religious nature as they accept candidly the results of historical evidence and scientific investigation, believing that all truth is of God.

Dr. Workman's book is an able as well as a useful exposition of the new line of defending the Scriptures by a man of ripe scholarship in the department with which it deals. It proceeds in what I believe to be the only safe and right direction for the reconciliation of religious faith with every other form of truth. The solution which the author gives is lucid in style, conservative in spirit, and constructive in aim. While it sacredly conserves the old truth, it fairly and frankly opens the mind to the new. It thus endeavors to interpret each in the light of the other, and so grasp them both in a true unity of thought.

As such a work, having such an aim, I heartily commend the volume to the serious consideration, not only of the Methodist Church, but also of the Christian public, as a valuable contribution to the elucidation of the Old Testament.

N. BURWASH.

TORONTO, April, 1897.

THE OLD TESTAMENT VINDICATED.

CHAPTER I.

ESSAY.

In the *North American Review* for December, 1895, there appeared from the pen of Professor Goldwin Smith an article,[1] entitled "Christianity's Millstone," which made considerable stir throughout the continent, and in some communities created a sensation. The striking form of the title challenged the attention of thoughtful people, and the sacred nature of the subject caused many persons to open the magazine with some uneasiness, if not with some concern.

Dr. Smith is a practised writer, as well as an accomplished scholar, and, like everything else that he writes, this contribution to religious

---

[1] Now published under another name, "The Church and the Old Testament," in a volume of essays, entitled "Guesses at the Riddle of Existence."

literature furnishes suggestive and instructive reading; but, interesting and stimulating as his paper is to read, his treatment of the Old Testament, with which his essay deals, is disappointing and unsatisfactory.

His criticism is sometimes severe, but his spirit is always reverent, and he never ridicules. Still, without disparaging it, or speaking slightingly of it, he makes the Old Testament appear to a disadvantage, and he makes the Church's use of it look ridiculous as well.

One is so accustomed to unfavorable criticism of the Bible that one comes to expect such criticism from a certain class of writers, but one can scarcely help feeling surprised that a scholar of such distinction would use the prestige of his name and fame in writing to the prejudice of the Old Testament. A man as familiar as Dr. Smith is with the principles of criticism might have been expected to apply them impartially, at least.

Had he employed his great ability in setting forth its qualities, or in making known its merits, instead of analyzing its ancient narratives to their disadvantage, he might have rendered an important service to the cause of truth. As it is, however, he has chosen to do a work, not of construction, but of demolition, by exhibiting its imperfections rather than its excellences.

One object of the essayist, so far as his article discovers his purpose, was, apparently, to foster a more rational view of the Bible, which is certainly a consummation devoutly to be wished; but the way in which he has sought to accomplish his object, if such really was his object, is extraordinary. He does not attempt to elucidate or explain the ancient Scriptures, but rather offers, in an attractive form, objections to them; and, in criticising their contents, he utterly ignores the modern evangelical method of interpreting the Bible.

Were a Biblical critic to discuss history as this critic, who is an adept in history, discusses Scripture, the distinguished historian would undoubtedly complain of unfairness, if not of incompetence. No impartial scientist would treat the subjects of his department, or suffer them to be treated, as Professor Smith has treated the writings of the Old Testament.

The objections contained in his essay are old and familiar, as a careful analysis of them will show. Most of them are connected with traditional views of Scripture such as were held by conservative teachers in the days of Dr. Buckland, whose lectures the essayist tells us he attended when a student at college.

This whole article, indeed, deals with a state of things which does not exist among thinking men to-day, and which has not existed amongst intelligent students of the Bible for, at least, a quarter of a century. "A more crude and unreasonable utterance upon the Old Testament," as Dr. George Adam Smith says, "has seldom issued from the press."[1]

Feeling that he has used the results of Biblical criticism in such a manner as to reflect on Biblical scholarship; fearing that his essay will exert a disturbing influence on the faith of some, as well as produce a false impression on

---

[1] A lecture delivered at the University of Chicago during the summer of 1896.

the minds of others, and believing that such a partial and one-sided treatment of Scripture should not remain unchallenged, lest the enemies of Christianity should conclude that it cannot be fairly answered, the present writer has been impelled, in the interest of religious truth, to publish a complete answer to all his principal objections.

CHAPTER II.

OCCASION.

THE occasion of this elaborate essay was the publication of an address, delivered before the members of the then recent English Church Congress at Norwich, England, by Professor Bonney, Canon of Manchester, who made a few unhappy remarks respecting the true character of certain parts of the Old Testament, which Dr. Smith considers "a bold and honorable attempt to cast a millstone off the neck of Christianity by frankly renouncing belief in the historical character of the earlier books of the Bible."

"I cannot deny," said Canon Bonney, "that the increase of scientific knowledge has deprived parts of the earlier books of the Bible of the historical value which was generally attributed to them by our forefathers. The story of the creation in Genesis, unless we play fast and loose either with words or with science, cannot be brought into harmony with what we have learned from geology. Its ethnological statements are imperfect, if not sometimes inaccurate. The stories of the Flood and of the Tower of Babel are incredible in their present form. Some historical element may underlie many of the traditions in the first eleven chapters of that book, but this we cannot hope to recover."

Taking as a text this statement, which indicates rather a confused faith than an intelligent abandonment of faith, Dr. Smith reads between the lines what does not stand upon the lines by suggesting that, in order consistently to make such an acknowledgment, the author of it must renounce certain unworthy conceptions of doctrine which there is no reason to suppose he holds, and which his fellow-workers in the field of Biblical criticism most assuredly do not hold.

"With the historical character of the chapters relating to the creation," says the essayist, "Canon Bonney must resign his belief in the Fall of Adam; with his belief in the Fall of

Adam he must surrender the doctrine of the Atonement, as connected with that event, and thus relieve conscience of the strain put upon it in struggling to reconcile vicarious punishment with our sense of justice. He will also have to lay aside his belief in the Serpent of the Temptation, and in the primeval personality of Evil."

Professor Smith is too profound a student, general as well as special, not to know that the account of the Fall in Genesis, which was once explained by theologians as literal history, is now explained by Christian scholars as religious allegory—an allegory, like a parable, being a form of narrative employed by the sacred writers to illustrate and inculcate spiritual truth.

The second and third chapters of the book were constructed out of traditional materials which are not only of Babylonian origin, but are also stamped with a Babylonian impress, as Professor Sayce, the eminent archæologist, has shown.[1] Hence, in primitive times, no doubt,

---

[1] "The Higher Criticism and the Monuments," Chap. III.

some features of the story were regarded as literal facts which, at the present time, are not so regarded; but the structure of the narrative indicates that the inspired writer purposely clothed his description of the Garden, as well as his account of the Fall, in somewhat symbolic language.

This latter portion of Scripture is an allegorical or a parabolical representation of the beginning of moral evil in human nature. As "a sublime allegory of the birth of conscience," it describes what happens in the experience of men to-day as truly as it describes what happened in man's experience at the dawn of history. Whenever or however sin first appeared on the earth, the story of the Fall of Adam is based upon a fact as universal as the race, a fact to which the common conscience of mankind bears witness. Sin *has* entered into the world, and spiritual death, or separation from God, has been the result.

Interpreted in harmony with its figurative style, the account contains neither irrational doctrine nor unhistoric fact. Inasmuch as the doctrine of a personal devil does not belong to Mosaism, and does not appear in the Old Testament before the time of the Exile, the best interpreters of Genesis do not hold that the story of the Fall teaches the primeval personality of Evil. "The story apparently presupposes an ungodly principle which had already entered the world," says Oehler, "but does not give any further account of it."[1]

Inasmuch, too, as the serpent was used, from prehistoric times throughout the East, as an emblem of an evil principle, or a spirit of disobedience and contumacy, in the world, a true interpretation of the account does not require us to believe in the actual appearance of a tempting serpent. Hence, as we are not to understand that a real serpent ever tempted any one to sin, the narrative teaches, amongst other things, that man fell into sin at first, as he falls into sin now, by consciously yielding to temptation—in other words, through the voluntary transgression of known law.

While Paul uses the familiar form of Genesis

---

[1] "Theology of the Old Testament," Am. edition, p. 158.

in introducing the doctrine of Atonement, and, in that sense, connects it with the Fall of Adam, the apostle really connects the doctrine with the entrance of sin as a moral fact into human nature. Consequently, we are not required by anything in the Bible "to reconcile vicarious punishment with our sense of justice," as Dr. Smith suggests, because the New Testament writers nowhere represent our heavenly Father as punishing Christ for the sins of men. They simply represent our Lord as, in loving obedience to the will of his Father, effecting the reconciliation of man to God.

It is true that Bishop Butler speaks of the sacrifice of Christ as a "vicarious punishment," but he employs the words, not in the sense of an inflictive penalty exacted or imposed by God, but in the sense of "a providential appointment of every day's experience." "In the daily course of natural providence," he says, "it is appointed that innocent people should suffer for (on account of) the faults of the guilty."[1] He further says that as "one person's sufferings

[1] "Complete Works," p. 181.

contribute to the relief of another," so "the sufferings of Christ could contribute to the redemption of the world." Vicarious punishment, however, is an ambiguous as well as an unscriptural expression, which should never be applied to the redemptive work of Christ.

CHAPTER III.

METHOD.

The method which the essayist has adopted is peculiar. Assuming that Biblical inspiration is equivalent to dictation by the Holy Spirit (a theory which no scholar holds), he shows that the Old Testament contains some things which are incompatible with such a view (a truism which no scholar doubts); and then he asks if these things are inspired (a supposition which no scholar entertains). He thus creates absurdities and inconsistencies that do not exist, except in the mind of one who holds distorted views of Scripture.

Pursuing this plan throughout his article, he presents, perhaps, the most misleading, if not the most mischievous, critique of the ancient Scriptures that has ever been written by a reverent religious scholar; so that to the superficial reader his essay seems like a formidable arraignment of the Old Testament, whereas it is simply an arraignment of an obsolete theory of the Old Testament. That is to say, he arraigns the well-known difficulties connected with an old-fashioned view of Scripture, which a recent, but truly evangelical, view removes.

The peculiar method which characterizes his essay is further illustrated by the strange way in which he treats the other fundamental questions of Biblical study, especially such questions as revelation, interpretation and citation. Though modern exegetes present a view of revelation that is both sensible and scriptural, though they employ a method of interpretation that is both scientific and critical, though they proclaim a principle of quotation that is both rational and evangelical, yet, in dealing with each of these features of the Bible, he is just as unfair as he is in dealing with its inspiration.

Biblical scholarship is not in such a deplorable condition as Dr. Smith's misleading article implies. It recognizes all the difficulties, moral, historical or theological, that really exist; but it sees a way by which, in every instance, the difficulty may be explained in harmony with the claims of Scripture, as well as with the claims of reason.

Moreover, modern scholars modify their views of the Bible, and improve their methods of interpreting it, according to the evidence furnished by the facts which it reveals, just as they modify their notions of the universe, and correct their theories respecting it, according to the testimony of the facts revealed in nature.

The writer of this remarkable critique is so familiar with the literature *on* the Bible, as well as with the literature *of* the Bible, that he could, doubtless, have answered many, if not most, of the objections which he urges against a traditional construction of Scripture, in harmony with a critical interpretation of it; but, instead of answering his own objections, or, instead of showing how they may be rationally and scripturally answered, he has employed the results of criticism to overthrow what are but the misconceptions of traditionalism.

As a clever journalist, in directing attention to

some strange features of his article, remarked, "He has taken the new learning to demolish an old position, and has said nothing of the way in which the new learning sees and traces the hand of God in the Old Testament."

To use the results of criticism, as Dr. Smith does, to arraign the misconceptions of traditionalism, without showing the elements of truth which the latter contained, is as unwarrantable as to take the established facts of chemistry to demolish the absurd superstitions of alchemy, without showing the important service which it rendered in the development of the more perfect science.

By such an unfair use of facts, a modern specialist could make almost any ancient department of knowledge look ridiculous; but no one would be justified in thus treating the false notions of a former age. Yet, notwithstanding its unfairness, such is the manner in which the writer of this strange critique has seen fit to perform his work. Besides employing a most unscientific method of studying the Scriptures, he has used the results of his study in a most unscientific way.

This essay, it should be said, shows reading, but neither investigation nor research; and, though skilful in execution, it is unsettling in tendency and destructive in aim. The essayist magnifies the teaching of sceptical writers and minimizes that of evangelical writers. All through his article, moreover, he proceeds on false assumptions. He also makes assertions and draws inferences that are quite unwarrantable. He has a habit, too, of interrogating and insinuating his objections, which tends as well to excite suspicion as to produce a wrong impression in regard to certain doctrines to which he is opposed.

While his criticisms deal in particular with the historical portions, they embrace in general all the special or distinctive features, of the Old Testament—its inspiration, its revelation, its evolution, its interpretation, its citation, its history, its patriarchs, its science, its religion, its morality, its barbarity, its sacrifice, its election, its anthropomorphism, its miracles, its prophecy, its immortality, its qualities.

CHAPTER IV.

INSPIRATION.

TREATING of certain mythical or traditional materials out of which the editor of *Lux Mundi* admits that some parts of the Old Testament were developed, the essayist says, "It is difficult to see how myths can in any sense be inspired, or why, if the records are in any sense inspired, the Church should not be able to insist on their historical character." He thus criticises the mechanical character of the Old Testament inspiration.

Dr. Smith should have noticed that, in his essay on "The Holy Spirit and Inspiration," the editor of *Lux Mundi*[1] does not assume that myths are inspired. He simply regards traditional narratives, such as those presented in the

[1] A volume of religious essays, edited by Dr. Charles Gore, Principal of Keble College, Oxford.

earlier chapters of Genesis, as containing "great inspirations about the origin of all things—the nature of sin, the judgment of God on sin, and the alienation among men which follows their alienation from God"—inspirations "conveyed to us in that form of myth or allegorical picture, which is the earliest mode in which the mind of man apprehended truth."[1]

The Church does not need to insist, and certainly does not intend to insist, on the historical character of any account that is not demonstrably historical. Such a policy would be as perilous as it would be unprincipled. But, while the Church does not claim that myths as such are in any sense inspired, she does claim that a religious man may have been inspired to use allegorical pictures, just as our Lord used parabolical descriptions, for the purpose of communicating moral and spiritual truth.

In the same connection, Dr. Smith asks, "Is it conceivable that the Holy Spirit, in dictating the record of God's dealings with mankind for our instruction in the way of life, should simu-

[1] Essay VIII., p. 298.

late the defects of human evidence?" when he knows very well that such a supposition is as unworthy as it is impossible, and as unscriptural as it is irrational. That which is defective or imperfect about the Bible was due, not to divine dictation, but to human limitation.

He knows, too, that no scholar of repute to-day accepts the "dictation" theory of inspiration, because, in the closing paragraph of his article, he very properly speaks of "verbal inspiration" as being but "a consecrated tradition." All such mechanical theories of the Bible have long since been discarded. The Holy Spirit did not dictate the words of Scripture, but inspired the spiritual ideas it contains. God dealt with the sacred writers, as he deals with us, not as machines, but as men.

He must also know that, instead of assuming that the Holy Spirit dictated the records of Scripture, or simulated the defects of human evidence in dictating them, the editor of the volume already mentioned expressly says that "the recorders of Israel's history were subject to the ordinary laws in the estimate of evidence," and that "their inspiration did not consist in a miraculous communication to them of facts as they originally happened."[1] The same editor had already said, "The inspiration of the recorder lies primarily in this, that he sees the hand of God in the history and interprets his purpose."

The Old Testament historians are said to have been inspired because they were moved by the Holy Spirit to trace the workings of God in history, and to interpret the dealings of God with men, not because they were miraculously informed concerning matters which did not come within the range of their experience.

As regeneration, or divine renewing, gives us no new knowledge of science or philosophy, so inspiration, or divine inbreathing, gave them no new knowledge of the facts of history. The Divine Spirit quickened their faculties in reference to spiritual, not temporal, things. Their inspiration thus consisted in their quickened insight into the ways of God, and their quickened foresight respecting his providential purpose.

[1] Essay VIII., p. 295.

The preceding paragraph indicates that inspiration properly applies to a person, not to a book, so that the word should be connected rather with the authors than with the books of Scripture. Nevertheless, the Bible may be called an inspired book, because it was written by men who were inspired of God to apprehend and communicate spiritual truth. Inasmuch, however, as it is simply the spiritual or divine element in it to which the term is applicable, Biblical inspiration refers exclusively to that element in the Scriptures.

That is to say, only the teaching in them which pertains to divine redemption, and deals with those ideas which have to do with faith and conduct, has the guarantee of inspiration. Respecting matters not pertaining to redemption, or not connected with salvation, Christian scholars claim for the inspired writers of Scripture only what such writers claim for themselves, namely, that they were prompted by the Holy Spirit to make an honest use of the best knowledge they possessed for the purpose of teaching religious truth.

While, therefore, the Scripture writers acted under a divine impulse in apprehending and communicating their religious ideas, we must not assume that every part of the Bible contains a divinely inspired statement, or expresses a divinely inspired sentiment. The sayings of ungodly men, the communications of false prophets, and the conversations of Satan prove the correctness of this assertion.

It is only the moral truths and spiritual principles of the Bible that are divinely inspired; and it is only these truths and principles taken together that constitute a trustworthy guide of life, and form a sufficient rule of practice. By applying the foregoing test, the divine element in the Scriptures may be readily discerned, and its presence or absence in any part of them as readily determined.

CHAPTER V.

REVELATION.

AFTER specifying some of the qualities that have given the books of the Old Testament, in spite of their primeval views on various subjects, so strong a hold on the allegiance of civilized minds, the essayist says, " The time has surely come when as a supernatural revelation they should be frankly, though reverently, laid aside." He thus criticises the supernatural character of the Old Testament revelation.

Professor Smith must surely know that the time has long come since the soundest Christian teachers taught that the Old Testament is not a revelation, but the record of a revelation. This distinction has been observed by evangelical writers for upwards of a score of years. Oehler, for instance, the author of one of the oldest and ablest works on Biblical theology, a work to be found in all the English and American colleges, emphatically says, "The Bible is not revelation itself; it is the record of revelation."[1]

In saying that the Bible is not a revelation, but the record of a revelation, theologians mean that revelation is not synonymous with the books of Scripture, and must not be confounded with them. In addition to the divine element contained in them, they contain a human element which is not a supernatural, but a purely natural, product.

The revelation in the Bible is the spiritual knowledge that has been transmitted to us from ancient times through the recorded utterances of inspired men on religious subjects. In other words, it is the knowledge of God which the record conveys to our minds. But, since all knowledge in the Bible is not divine knowledge, we get an adequate notion of the sacred Scriptures only when we realize that they are a collection of inspired writings—that is, an inspired literature which contains a divine revelation.

[1] "Theology of the Old Testament," Am. edition, p. 8.

The inspiration of the ancient Scriptures is not an invention of modern theology, but a doctrine of primitive Christianity. Referring to the prophetic portions of the Old Testament, one apostle says that "men spake from God, being moved by the Holy Spirit;"[1] and, speaking of those parts of the Old Testament which are able to make one wise unto salvation, another apostle declares that all such Scripture is "inspired of God."[2]

It seems unfortunate, however, that in past times men chose rather to speculate what the Bible ought to be than to examine what the Bible actually is. Instead of theorizing so much about the doctrine of inspiration, they should have shown the sense in which the Scripture writers claim to have been inspired, as well as the extent to which their utterances deal with moral and spiritual truth.

Owing to the existence of two elements in Scripture, the one a divine, the other a human element, the Bible is now acknowledged by all scholars to be the record of a revelation which

---

[1] 2 Peter i. 21. [2] 2 Tim. iii. 16.

was received, during a long period of time, by a large number of men, who spoke or wrote on religious subjects, as they were moved by the Holy Spirit, but who made use of a great variety of materials, traditional, historical and philosophical, according to the fullest light they had, and the soundest judgment they possessed.

Modern scholars not only distinguish between revelation and Scripture, but they also distinguish between revelation and inspiration. Inspiration is the inbreathing of the Divine Spirit upon the human spirit, whereas revelation is the unveiling of the divine mind to the human mind. Subjectively, the first is an impulse from God; the second, a manifestation of God. Objectively, the former is a state of soul; the latter, a view of truth. While both involve a supernatural act, the one is the process of an operation of which the other is the result. Inspiration qualified religious men to receive and communicate the supernatural information which constitutes revelation.

Strictly speaking, Biblical inspiration applies solely to the authors of Scripture, while Biblical revelation applies solely to the truths of Scripture. Hence we speak of an inspired man, but of a revealed truth. The Bible is called an inspired book, because it was written by inspired men; it is called a book of revelation, because it contains a record of revealed truth.

But all that is true in the Bible is not divine truth. Much of what is true in it is either human reflection or historic fact. For this reason, it would prevent confusion if, when referring to the Bible, we always spoke of inspiration as the influence of God exerted upon the writers of Scripture, and of revelation as the knowledge of God contained in Scripture.

Though he rejects the Hebrew Scriptures as a supernatural revelation in the obsolete sense which no modern scholar holds, yet, towards the conclusion of his article, the essayist grants that the Old Testament may, so far as it is good, be a manifestation of the Divine. "As a manifestation of the Divine," he says, "the Hebrew books, teaching righteousness and purity, may have their place in our love and admiration forever."

In making this admission, he substantially allows the very thing which Christian scholarship maintains; for, if these books are a manifestation of God, they must not only, in some sense, be an inspired literature, but also, in some degree, contain a divine revelation. It is because these books are an inspired literature that they teach righteousness and purity with such directness and authoritativeness; and it is because they contain a divine revelation that they will always elicit the love and admiration of mankind.

Every part of the Hebrew Scriptures is of use for some purpose, and has a value of some kind; but it is the incomparable divine element in them—that is, the special spiritual revelation they contain—which distinguishes them from all other ancient writings, and makes them of permanent doctrinal importance to the Church, as well as gives them a permanent devotional value to Christian people. Science can never lessen their importance, nor can criticism ever impair their value, for religious purposes.

CHAPTER VI.

EVOLUTION.

ASSUMING that the religion of the Israelites was originally the same as that of the other inhabitants of Canaan, the essayist represents the ascent of the Hebrew race from fetichism and nature-worship to an exalted type of monotheism as "a historical mystery." He thus criticises the mysterious character of the Old Testament evolution.

Everything connected with primeval ages is necessarily obscure, but not necessarily mysterious. On this account, it would be more correct to describe the way in which Abraham's progenitors, who, we are told, "served other gods,"[1] rose from polytheism to monotheism as obscure rather than mysterious; for, while we cannot trace the course by which the ancestors of Israel

[1] Josh. xxiv. 2.

advanced from one stage to another in their views of the Divine Being, we can explain the process by which their conceptions of his character were developed.

We know from experience that God's ordinary way of working is progressive. We know from experience, too, that man's only way of apprehending is gradual. Since all revelation is commensurate with the medium through which it is made, God's manifestation of himself to men depends partly on his law of evolution, and partly on their power of apprehension. We naturally infer, therefore, that man's knowledge of God in every age must have been governed by the law of gradual progress.

Our natural inference is corroborated by a comparative study of the Scriptures themselves. On examination, the Old Testament proves to be the record of such a spiritual evolution as experience leads us to infer. We can trace both progress and development in the revelation it contains. We actually find in it, too, a gradually advancing series of statements respecting the character of the Deity. Beginning with his more general characteristics, it presents one attribute after another, in what seems to have been the order in which primitive men perceived the Infinite manifesting himself in nature and in national life.

God is represented first as a creative Being,[1] next as an almighty Being,[2] next as a self-existent Being,[3] then as a holy Being,[4] and afterwards as an absolute Being.[5] The attribute of omnipotence does not appear in Scripture till the age of the patriarchs; the attribute of self-existence does not appear till the time of Moses; the attribute of holiness does not appear till the founding of the theocracy; the attribute of omnipresence does not appear till the period of the canonical prophets.

From the progressive development of the conception of the divine nature as exhibited in the Scriptures, we may safely assume the same sort of evolution for the ages before the Scriptures were produced, namely, a gradual ascent from fetichism and polytheism to the worship of a single God. As revelation is not simply a

---

[1] Gen. i. 1. [2] Gen. xvii. 1. [3] Exod. iii. 14.
[4] Lev. xi. 44. [5] Isa. xliv. 6.

gradual but a continuous process, there must have been a spiritual continuity of ideas in prehistoric times, just as there has been a spiritual continuity of ideas in historic times.

But, by what means, the essayist inquires, was this advancement made? Were the influences those of general circumstance, or those of individual reformers like the prophets? he desires to know. There were special circumstances, of course. The evolution of divine ideas is not a naturalistic, but a supernaturalistic, process. Judging from his dealings with his people in after ages, God must, from time to time, throughout primeval ages, have raised up men, elect men, chosen vessels, so to speak, who exercised the office, though they did not bear the name, of prophets.

Religion was a racial peculiarity of the Hebrews, as philosophy was of the Greeks, and as jurisprudence was of the Romans; but they had no such genius for the production of spiritual ideas as to warrant us in supposing that the monotheism of the Old Testament was a natural product of the ancient Semitic spirit. The unique religious development of the Hebrew people before the Bible, or any part of it, existed, proves that some of their ancestors in prehistoric times were specially influenced and enlightened by the Holy Spirit, because at the very dawn of history this people possessed a special knowledge, partial and imperfect as it was, of the one living and true God.

Though unknown to us, they must have been inspired of God, otherwise the knowledge which they obtained of him, and which they transmitted to their posterity, would have been impossible. For, as no men whose minds had not been specially subordinated to the Divine Spirit, could have raised morality and religion to the height to which they were raised by the canonical prophets, so no human beings whose faculties had not been energized and assisted by the Spirit of God, could have developed such a conception of the Deity as we find presented in the earliest books of the Old Testament.

The existence of monotheism prior to the existence of the Bible shows that revelations were received before the Scriptures were compiled. It also shows that revelations take place independently of the Bible. Being the outcome of a living continuous agency, they are occurring all the time. God is always unveiling himself and disclosing his secrets to the minds of devout men. Hence there is a sense in which revelation can never be a finished product.

We sometimes speak of the Christian revelation as final in the sense that it contains all truth essential to salvation; but, while no new truth respecting divine redemption has been revealed since the manifestation of God in Christ, man's views of truth have become more adequate, having increased in fulness and completeness from age to age. Man, indeed, is constantly getting a deeper insight into the ways of God, a greater knowledge of his works, a larger acquaintance with his laws, and, as a consequence, a better understanding of his perfect will.

CHAPTER VII.

INTERPRETATION.

REFERRING to an old-fashioned method of reading or studying the Scriptures, the essayist suggests that "the first step towards a rational appreciation of the Old Testament is to break up the volume, separate the acts of Joshua or Jehu from the teachings of Jesus, and the different books of the Old Testament from each other." He thus criticises the uncritical character of the Old Testament interpretation.

In giving this advice, the essayist must have been aware that what he so sagaciously proposes is just what Christian teachers are doing, and just what they have been doing for a great many years. For the sake of convenience, the Old Testament is sometimes put with the New Testament, and published with it in a single volume; but the two Testaments thus bound together are not then treated as one book.

Every teacher knows, and every student is given to understand, that the Bible is not a book, but a collection of books. That is to say, it is a body of religious literature, the New Testament being the sacred writings of the Christians, the Old Testament being the sacred writings of the Jews. Hence the one group is often called the Christian Scriptures; the other group, the Jewish Scriptures.

The Old Testament is, as Dr. Smith himself remarks, "the entire body of Hebrew literature, theology, philosophy, history, fiction, and poetry, including the poetry of love as well as that of religion." Being a literature that was gradually developed through the action of the Divine Spirit on the minds of godly men, scholars recognize not only that it contains a great variety of matter, but also that it reveals a great diversity of purpose.

While they observe that the bulk of this literature possesses a religious character, and was written with a religious purpose, they likewise observe that some of it has a historical purpose, some of it a chronological purpose, some of it a biographical purpose, some of it a genealogical purpose, some of it a prophetic purpose, some of it a sanitary purpose, some of it a national purpose, like the book of Esther, some of it a patriotic purpose, like the book of Lamentations, and some of it a moral purpose, like the Song of Songs.

Modern teachers, it may thus be seen, do not put all the books of the Bible on the same level, or attach to all parts of it the same importance. They admit that every book in the Canon has a certain value, and was written for a worthy object, or with a worthy purpose; but they do not regard the whole contents of Scripture as possessing an equal value, or as having an identical purpose. They claim neither that the Song of Solomon is as spiritually edifying as are the Psalms of David, nor that the genealogies of Genesis are as divinely authoritative as is the Gospel of Christ.

Moreover, when expounding the Scriptures, Christian exegetes no longer adopt apologetic and dogmatic methods of interpretation, which proceed upon hypothetical or dogmatic assumptions, but a critical and scientific method, known as the historical method, which seeks in every case to ascertain what meaning the words of a writer were intended to convey at the time when they were written; and which shows in many cases that a passage that was once understood in a literal signification, was not intended to be taken literally by the person that wrote it, or by the Spirit that inspired it.

Adopting this truly rational method, which is now employed in studying ancient documents of every kind, an exegete, before interpreting any passage, always desires to know first what kind of literature it is, and secondly what sort of purpose it reveals. Having determined the character of the composition, and having discovered the purpose of the author, he interprets the passage in harmony with the laws which govern that particular kind of literature, whether it be history or allegory, prophecy or philosophy, poetry or prose.

It is by the application of this improved literary method, the principles of which are sanctioned by the soundest evangelical interpreters throughout the world, that the true character of the early chapters of Genesis, the book of Jonah, the book of Daniel, and many other difficult parts of the Old Testament, have at length been ascertained.

In view of these well-known facts, it seems very unfair of the essayist to say that " we have forcibly turned Hebrew literature into a sort of cryptogram of Christianity," as if he believed respectable scholarship was still pursuing such a foolish course. It is a good while since the Song of Songs, which all reputable scholars now regard as a lyric poem intended to display the triumph of pure affection over the temptations of wealth and rank, has been turned by intelligent interpreters into "a cryptogrammic description of the union of Christ with his Church."

The spiritualizing of Scripture for the sake of obtaining a Christian meaning, or with a view of solving a moral difficulty, is as unscientific as it is unauthorized, and such a practice is not countenanced by any competent expositor. No part of the Bible should be treated as an allegory, unless it proves on examination to be allegorical both in structure and in purpose; nor should any passage of the Old Testament be applied to Christ simply because it fancifully seems to fit him, but because it prophetically refers to him and consistently describes some incident in his life or some feature of his work.

Before the employment of a critical method in studying the Bible, the Song of Songs was commonly treated as an allegory, because of the peculiarity of its language, so much of which was capable of being interpreted in an allegorical signification. But, while there is a difference of opinion amongst expositors respecting some details of the book, owing to the construction of the poem and the distribution of its parts, all modern scholars recognize that the poetry is not only lyrical in character, but also dramatic in form. Perceiving that the Song is essentially a drama, with a rudimentary kind of plot, they also perceive that it contains an exquisite description of the constant devotion of a Shulamite maiden to her shepherd lover.

Though the poem has not the mystical significance it was once supposed to have, and does not in any way refer either to Christ or to his Church, it, nevertheless, reveals a truly moral purpose, having been manifestly written with a view of celebrating loyal love in lowly life. It is fitting that one book in the Bible should be devoted to the glorification of pure and faithful love—"a love which," as one has said, "no splendor can dazzle and no flattery seduce."

CHAPTER VIII.

CITATION.

DESCRIBING the way in which our Lord used the sacred writings of his people, the essayist first assumes that the book of Jonah is an apologue, and then he asserts that the Great Teacher cites it "in terms which seem to show that he regards it as a real history." He thus criticises the inconsistent character of the Old Testament citation.

If the book of Jonah is an apologue, as the essayist assumes, or a prophetic parable, as many modern exegetes maintain, why should he insinuate that Jesus seems to regard it as a real history? By this insinuation he virtually impeaches the veracity as well as the authority of Christ. Such an impeachment is inexcusable.

Does Dr. Smith not know that Jesus, like the apostles, made a strictly religious use of the Old

Testament? Having used it solely with a religious aim, he did not stop to discuss the literary character of its books; so that it is not necessary to impeach either his authority or his veracity, in order consistently to explain his reference to any book in harmony with the results of Christian criticism.

Our Lord cited the Old Testament for purely practical purposes, as well as with a purely religious aim; and he referred to its books just as the representatives of the Church in his day referred to them. Had he spoken of their Scriptures in any other way, the people whom he taught would not have understood him, or have apprehended what he meant.

Since Jesus made a practical, not a critical, use of the Old Testament, he does not tell us, by alluding to a well-known narrative like the one under consideration, whether the adventure with the fish is a literary incident or a historical event. Hence it is as unwarrantable for men to claim that his reference to the story of Jonah proves that the incident is historical, or that he believed it to be historical, as it is for them to claim that his allusion to the phenomenon of sunrising[1] proves that the conception is scientific, or that he meant it to be scientific.

We now know that the sun does not rise, but merely seems to rise; we likewise have the best of reasons for believing that the story of Jonah is not literal but tropical history. Therefore, believers have no more right to conclude from our Lord's didactic use of the story that he regarded it as real history, than sceptics have to conclude from his popular use of the notion of sunrising that he regarded such a notion as sound science.

In claiming that the story of Jonah is not literal but tropical history, Christian scholars do not deny that Jonah was a real personage, or that the outlines of the narrative rest upon a basis of fact; but, besides seeing that some features of the story are not to be taken literally, they see other indications that the narrative is not strictly historical. The book was evidently written with a distinctly didactic pur-

---

[1] Matt. v. 45.

pose; and, irrespective of its literary character, the lessons included in it are quite plain. Whether the original materials of the narrative were chiefly parabolical or chiefly historical, it clearly teaches that God's purposes of grace are not limited to a single people, and that a duty divinely imposed upon a prophet, or upon any other person, ought not to be evaded, and cannot be evaded with impunity.

From the way in which he alluded to the phenomenon of sunrising we may see that Christ employed the common forms of human speech, and spoke to men in such a manner as to be readily understood by them. The Gospel record shows not only that he discussed religious questions in the ordinary language of his time, but also that he referred to familiar subjects of every kind in accordance with the conceptions which then prevailed.

Our Lord's references to the Old Testament give us no information whatever about the critical issues connected with its books, because they amount to nothing more than popular modes of expression, or accepted forms of speech.

Hence his utterance in the New Testament regarding any Old Testament book does not raise, much less decide, the question either of its age, or of its authorship, or of its literary character.

As reverent students of the Bible, we should be careful not to attribute to Jesus views on any subject concerning which he does not bear explicit testimony. We should also be careful not to claim, without an express warrant, his supreme authority as deciding questions which the Divine Being has left to be determined by inquiry or research. It has been shown, however, that Jesus expressed no judgment at all respecting matters of history or science. For this reason, we are not warranted at all in referring to him as an authority in any such matters.

On those themes which pertain to salvation, he speaks to us with divine authority as the way, the truth, and the life of men; but he leaves all questions of historical or literary criticism, such as the composite origin of the Pentateuch, the allegoric character of the account of the Fall, and the parabolic character of the book of Jonah, to be settled by study and investigation, just as the sacred writers of the Old Testament left the great problems of physical and astronomical science to be settled in the same way.

Inasmuch as the argument he used, or the comparison he made, or the lesson he taught, or the principle he applied, was always truly contained in the Scripture he quoted, it follows that he could consistently cite a familiar passage from the books of the Psalms, or from the books of the Law, without expressing any judgment respecting their authorship; and that he could just as consistently employ a suggestive incident, such as the symbolic event recorded in the book of Jonah, as an illustration for his special typical purpose without giving, or intending to give, any opinion whatsoever as to whether the narrative in question was history or allegory, or a blending of both.

CHAPTER IX.

HISTORY.

DISSECTING the mythical or traditional features of the subject-matter of the book of Genesis, the essayist says, "The history of every nation begins with myth. A primeval tribe keeps no record, and a nation in its maturity has no more recollection of what happened in its infancy than a man of what happened to him in his cradle." He thus criticises the untrustworthy character of the Old Testament history.

This statement is unquestionably true, but its implication is misleading. A myth is not a falsehood, much less an imposture. It is a presentation of truth in fictitious or rather tropical form. As the editor of *Lux Mundi* says, "It is a product of mental activity, as instructive and rich as any later product, but its characteristic is that it is not yet distinguished into history, and poetry, and philosophy. It is all of these in the germ, as dream and imagination, and thought and experience, are fused in the mental furniture of a child's mind."[1]

The narratives of Genesis, however, cannot properly be called myths. The earlier ones express the world's best traditional conceptions, at the time when they were compiled, respecting the origins of things; and they embody, in tropical form, not only important historic facts, but also great moral and religious truths. Having passed through the purifying fire of the true religious spirit of inspiration, they were placed by the compiler as the introduction to the history of the Hebrew people. Owing to their age and character, though, it should not be claimed for either the earlier or the later narratives of the Pentateuch that they furnish a perfect modern scientific ethnology, chronology, cosmogony, or synopsis of history, although from them each of these subjects may have derived important aid.

[1] Essay VIII., p. 297.

Canon Bonney's admission, therefore, which Dr. Smith considers so significant, that "the increase of scientific knowledge has deprived parts of the earlier books of the Bible of the historical value which was generally attributed to them by our forefathers," though made in language that seems to imply doubt and tends to create surprise, is one which does not at all involve the essayist's conclusions. Our forefathers thought that the first part of Genesis was the oldest piece of literature in existence; but the recent decipherment of the cuneiform inscriptions has revealed another still more ancient literature, one which gives us an Assyrian account of the Creation, the Fall, the Flood, and the Tower of Babel, in a form that is shown by its mythological and polytheistic features to be much older than the Biblical account, the latter being a purified and spiritualized and monotheized version of the former. These things our forefathers did not know, because they had no means of knowing them.

Christian scholars have recognized for a long time that the ethnological statements of the book of Genesis are imperfect, just as they have recognized that the genealogical tables of the Evangelists are incomplete; but they do not suppose that such matters were dictated by the Holy Spirit. On the contrary, holding, as already shown, that it is the divine and not the human element in the Bible which is inspired, they also hold that the writers of Scripture gathered their historic materials in the ordinary way. That is to say, they collected their facts as fully as their opportunities permitted, and reported them as accurately as their knowledge would allow. None of the historians of the Bible claim exceptional enlightenment in regard either to the collection of facts or to the narration of events.

Evangelical scholars have long recognized, too, that the stories of the Flood and the Tower of Babel are characterized by a manner of expression which must be interpreted according to the habit of Oriental speech, and that they contain traditional elements which are peculiar to all such ancient accounts. Both stories, doubtless, have a historical basis, though each narrative was developed, as all students of Biblical literature know, from a common Semitic tradition; but this latter fact does not lessen the value of either story as a primitive means of imparting religious instruction. Each narrative clearly teaches that God regards either with favor or with disfavor the conduct of every human being—the account of the Flood showing that he rewards piety and punishes impiety, the account of the Confusion of Tongues showing the impossibility of thwarting his design respecting the diffusion of mankind throughout the earth.

When Dr. Smith complains in the language of the editor of *Lux Mundi* that "the Church cannot insist upon the historical character of the earliest records of the ancient Church in detail as she can on the historical character of the Gospels or the Acts of the Apostles," it is sufficient to reply that the Church does not insist, and does not think of insisting, upon the perfect historicity of those ancient narratives which are known to contain traditional elements, and which are also known to have been compiled long after the events recorded are said to have taken place.

She frankly admits that, previous to the time at which Abraham is believed to have emigrated with his family into Palestine, we cannot determine with certainty much of the history or the chronology pertaining to the primeval and patriarchal ages, because so little of the early record can be traced to a period at all approaching the events. About the time of Abraham, however, both the history and the chronology become more definitely determinable; so that, from this time onward, the vital features of the Biblical account may be consistently regarded as substantially historical.

Again, when he dissects the same editor's admission that the books of Chronicles represent not only "a later and less historical version of Israel's history than that given in Samuel and Kings," but also "the version of that history which had become current in the priestly schools," one need simply say that every competent scholar to-day would make a similar admission.

All Old Testament students know that the books of Chronicles, which are in some respects a supplement to the books of Kings, were written at a comparatively late date, and from a distinctively religious and Levitical point of view. Having been constructed with a purely didactic purpose, the narratives are colored by a religious theory, which shows that they were not intended to be studied as a mere historical compend, or abstract of facts. They have some historical value; but their chief importance is of an ecclesiastical and institutional character.

The books of the Chronicles illustrate the new homiletic method of treating history which began to prevail a few centuries before Christ. In them we have, as Professor Sayce says, "the first beginnings of that transformation of history into Haggadah (homiletic exegesis), which is so conspicuous in later Jewish literature."[1]

The main object of the Chronicler was not so much to write a history of his nation, as to impress the inspiring lessons which he conceived its history to teach; and the "idealizing" feat-

---

[1] "The Higher Criticism and the Monuments," p. 465.

ures of his work, to which the essayist refers, were neither "mythical" nor "unconscious" features, but conscious didactic representations, reflecting the spirit of his age, and designed to subserve the religious interests of the people for whom he wrote.

CHAPTER X.

PATRIARCHS.

CHARACTERIZING Abraham, Isaac and Jacob as "mythical founders of a race," the essayist declares that "the chapters relating to them are full of what, in an ordinary sense, would be called ethnological myth." He thus criticises the unreal character of the Old Testament patriarchs.

In thus declaring that the patriarchs are mythical creations, having no historical basis, Dr. Smith asserts what Scripture contradicts and archæology disproves. Every ancient nation has incorporated legendary and traditional elements with its early records, so that we should not look for scientific accuracy in the work of any one who collects and sifts the crude materials of a primitive age.

Recognizing the fragmentary and imperfect

character of the patriarchal sections of Genesis, evangelical interpreters, like Delitzsch and Dillmann, frankly admit that the narratives of the patriarchs belong rather to the realm of tradition than to the sphere of rigid history. We may confidently affirm, however, that the patriarchs must have lived and performed extraordinary deeds, "because otherwise," as Ewald says, "there would be no accounting for the rise of the existing traditions respecting them."[1]

But, while these narratives are admittedly traditional, the most important statements in them seem to be in the strictest sense historical, having apparently been based upon trustworthy reminiscences. The record reveals no trace of any purpose on the part of the compiler to invent superhuman characters, or to ascribe to them superhuman attributes. He speaks of the patriarchs as historical individuals, not as mythical personages; and he refers to certain events in their lives, not as popular legends, but as actual facts.

[1] "History of Israel," Vol. I., p. 300.

Moreover, archæological discovery enables us to test many of the historical statements of the Pentateuch, and monumental evidence enables us to prove that some of the narratives contained in it are derived from documents contemporaneous with the events they record. "Contemporaneous monuments are continually coming to light," says Professor Sayce, "which prove that in the story of the patriarchs and of the exodus we have truth and not legend."[1] Thus the monuments of Egypt, Armenia and Assyria are verifying, in a wonderful way, the general truthfulness of the Biblical account.

Because the story of Abraham is specially characterized by anthropomorphic and miraculous features, which are fully discussed in later chapters of this book, Professor Smith unreasonably concludes that the whole account must be relegated to the domain of tribal fancy. "It is a rule of criticism," he says, "that we cannot by any critical alembic extract materials for history out of fable. If the details of a story are fabulous, so is the whole." If all

[1] *Contemporary Review*, October, 1895.

the details of a story are fabulous, we cannot, of course, extract materials for history out of them; but, if the leading facts of a story are authentic, the general truth of it is guaranteed. As Dr. Smith himself observes, "Human testimony may sometimes fail in minor particulars, while in the main account of the matter it is true."

This seems to be the case in reference to the story of the patriarchs in general and of Abraham in particular. The name Abram has been found in cuneiform characters on early Babylonian contract-tablets, and the authenticity of important events in the life of the old patriarch is being vindicated from year to year by oriental archæology. The account of the military campaign described in the fourteenth chapter of Genesis, an account which bears internal proofs of historical accuracy, as Ewald contended half a century ago, has recently been confirmed by the testimony of Assyriology; and still more recently the name of Arioch, king of Ellasar, of Chedorlaomer, king of Elam, and of Tidal, king of nations, has been discovered.

Furthermore, the names of peoples and places contemporary with the patriarch are being verified by Assyriological research. All these discoveries possess the greatest possible importance. So far as their testimony goes, it proves not only that the reputed ancestor of the Hebrew people was a veritable historic personage, as the sacred writers teach, but also that the narration in Genesis gives us a true picture of real life in Palestine at the very time when he is said to have lived there.

Such remarkable confirmations of the Pentateuchal record, at the very points at which it touches contemporaneous records, warrant us in supposing that there is a solid substratum of history underlying the story of Abraham, as well as that of Isaac and Jacob—for the latter name, like that of Joseph, has also been found on the Babylonian tablets. Though at present we have not so much corroborative testimony concerning the two later patriarchs as we have concerning the earlier one, we have abundant reason, none the less, to believe in the reality of their lives, as the compilers of the Pentateuch declare, the extreme historical critics to the contrary notwithstanding.

The explorations now in progress also warrant us in assuming that still more light may be shed upon the history of the patriarchal period by the ancient monuments, and that they will yet bear further witness to the vital truths embodied in Biblical account. Archæological investigation has already done so much to accredit the truthfulness of those portions of the Old Testament which can be checked by contemporary history that it may be confidently expected in the not distant future to do a good deal more.

CHAPTER XI.

SCIENCE.

HAVING mentioned several times the crude conceptions of the Mosaic cosmogony, which he thinks irreconcilable with the facts of geology, the essayist says, "The Old Testament is altogether geocentric, and not merely in the phenomenal sense." He thus criticises the popular character of the Old Testament science.

That the Mosaic cosmogony represents the earth and not the sun as the centre of the universe, that it regards the heavenly bodies simply as they appear to a person standing on the earth, and that it describes only those functions which these bodies perform in relation to the earth, are facts familiar to the most superficial reader of the Bible; but no fair-minded person thinks of blaming Moses for this geocentric view, much less of holding him responsible for it. Up to a few centuries ago, the whole world held substantially the same view of the universe, and the great majority of men believed that the earth was flat, as well as that the sun revolved about it.

Like every other Scripture writer, the compiler of the book of Genesis shared the scientific conceptions of the age in which he lived, and wrote in harmony with the ideas which then prevailed, just as our Lord expressed his teaching in language corresponding to the scientific notions of his time, when he spoke of the sun rising "on the evil and the good."[1] The writer does not profess to give us a miraculous history of creation, nor does the Church claim that he anticipated in any way the results of modern discovery. Since the days of Kepler and Newton we have known, from demonstrable evidence, the true system of the universe; but, before the laws of the heavenly bodies were discovered, such a knowledge was impossible.

Supposing the story of creation to be a miraculously revealed account of the origin of

[1] Matt. v. 45.

all created objects, theologians once believed that the whole universe was constructed piece by piece, that the first man was made directly from the dust of the ground, and that the first woman was built out of a rib taken from his side. They once believed, too, that the world was formed in six days of twenty-four hours each, and that the earth was just four thousand years old at the birth of Christ.

Having obtained a better understanding of the literary construction of the story, as well as a clearer perception of the didactic purpose of the compiler, theologians now recognize that some features of the story are not to be treated literally, but tropically; and they also recognize that the aim of the writer was not to explain how anything actually came into being, or to tell how long the process of creation lasted, much less to give a complete history of our planet from the beginning, but rather to show that everything owes its existence to the creative energy of God, and to describe the divine adaptation of the earth to be the abode of creatures such as can subsist upon it.

With this twofold aim, impelled by a religious motive, the author of the first chapter of Genesis gives, for his time, a remarkably accurate account of the general order of creation, as well as a remarkably consistent scheme of the progressive development of the solar system. For his didactic purpose, he adopts, with certain modifications, the cosmogony that was common to the ancient world, a cosmogony that corresponded to the conceptions of those who, in the infancy of science, attempted to explain the physical phenomena of the universe.

Hence Christian scholars of the present day do not "play fast and loose either with words or with science," in order to bring the story of creation "into harmony with what we have learned from geology." They simply take the story for what it is, namely, a popular presentation of the more striking phenomena of creation for the purpose of teaching, not science or philosophy, in the technical sense of these terms, but moral and spiritual truth. They feel under no obligation to harmonize an ancient popular description with a modern systematized account.

In broad outline, they recognize that there is a substantial agreement between the narrative in Genesis and the teaching of science; and that is all we should expect, as well as all the Scripture, properly expounded, leads us to expect.

But, while the general order of Genesis is such as physical science now accepts, judicious teachers do not maintain that the narrative in the first chapter of the book is perfect geology. They perceive that the writer confined his account simply to the great facts of nature as he saw it, and that he expressed himself in language corresponding to what he saw. They also perceive that his description of the Spirit's operations as so many creative acts, occupying so many solar days, though having a general foundation in nature, merely represents an orderly progress in the work of creation.

Instead of claiming, therefore, that the story of creation coincides, in all respects, with the results which physical investigation has disclosed, the wisest teachers, recognizing the popular and picturesque character of the account, do not attempt to correlate Genesis and geology day by day. The compiler of Genesis was not thinking of geologic ages or geologic epochs. Such terms belong to geology, as a developed science, and were not invented till a comparatively recent date. The ordinary word for day employed by the writer is taken to represent the unknown time of one or, possibly, of more than one creative operation.

Since the story of creation is pictured rather than historically narrated—the week of creation having been modelled on the Jewish week in order to give a special sanctity to the Jewish Sabbath, as well as to present a general order of creative operation—the division of the creative period into six creative days of ordinary length belongs simply to the literary form of the account; and, since the account itself is tropical, the record tells us nothing whatever about the age of the world, the origin of matter, or the antiquity of man.

In a pregnant statement, at once the simplest and profoundest that had ever been uttered in so many words up to his day, the writer prefaces his narrative with the great religious announcement that everything was produced at some time or other by the creative power of a personal God. "In the beginning" (whenever that was), he says, "God" (in what manner or during what cycles does not appear) "created the heaven and the earth." He thus shows that the universe, which pagan nations deified, is the product of a divine mind.

Seeing that the first chapter of Genesis teaches neither geology nor chronology, there is nothing in it inconsistent with the doctrine of evolution that the world was formed by a gradual process of development in harmony with natural laws, or with the declaration of geology that animal life existed for ages before the human race appeared. That all created things are due to divine activity, and that spiritual death, or separation from God, is the outcome of human disobedience—these are two fundamental facts which the story of creation teaches, and which the testimony of the rocks does not gainsay.

Thus Christian geologists are not driven to the desperate shifts to which Professor Smith remembers that Dr. Buckland "was driven in his efforts to reconcile the facts of his science with the Mosaic cosmogony, the literal truth of which he did not venture to impugn." They rather deprecate the practice of forcing meanings out of Scripture in order to meet some supposed need of science, regarding it as both ridiculous and reprehensible.

No competent instructor now finds anything in the story of creation to impugn, since, technically speaking, the account is neither scientific nor unscientific, but non-scientific. The cosmogony adopted by the writer, though semi-scientific in character, was used by him, not for the purpose of teaching science, but for the purpose of teaching religion. Much less does any wise apologist try to reconcile the facts of science with the doctrines of Scripture, because, if science be fairly expounded and Scripture be rightly interpreted, there is no conflict or antagonism between them. The book of Genesis gives us no theory, in the modern use of the term, either of the process of creation or of the origin of the world; it merely connects God with creation in an order founded upon the best conceptions of nature to which the mind of man had then attained.

CHAPTER XII.

RELIGION.

REGARDING the Hebrew religion as a tribal monotheism, although, as he admits, a tribal monotheism of an eminently pure and exalted type, the essayist asserts that "higher than to tribal monotheism it did not rise." He thus criticises the national character of the Old Testament religion.

This assertion is singularly inconsistent with the facts of the Old Testament. The religion of Israel started as a tribal monotheism, but it rose to an ethical monotheism, the germ of which goes back to very remote times. That is to say, the idea of a tribal Deity who has a special relation to a single people, developed, with the religious progress of the nation, into the idea of an absolute Deity who has moral relations with every people. Jehovah, it should be noted, was the name "by which," as Professor Sayce observes, "the national God of the Hebrews was distinguished from the gods of the heathen."[1]

In the teaching of the prophets, there is a manifest advance upon the teaching of the Pentateuch respecting the doctrine of God—an advance towards a clearer perception, not of his personality, but of his universality. A comparative study of the ancient Scriptures shows that, while the conception of Jehovah as a living moral person is as distinctly set forth in the earlier as in the later books of the Old Testament, an enlarged conception of his relation to the world is presented in the writings of the prophets.

By Isaiah and the teachers that succeeded him, Jehovah is no longer regarded as the God of one nation only, but as the mighty Sovereign of the universe, who rules in the realm of nature and overrules in the sphere of history. Many passages might be quoted to show that Israelism or Israelitism, which commenced as a national religion, restricted in some measure to

---

[1] "The Higher Criticism and the Monuments," p. 87.

a single nation, developed, with the progress of revelation, into a universal religion which knows no national limitations, because it rests upon belief in a Supreme Being who is the Saviour of all the ends of the earth.

On account of its fulness and completeness, one verse from the book of Nehemiah will be sufficient for the present purpose. Referring to the supreme majesty and omnipotence of Jehovah, the speaker exclaims, "Thou hast made heaven, the heaven of heavens, with all their host, the earth and all things that are thereon, the seas and all that is in them, and thou preservest them all; and the host of heaven worshippeth thee."[1]

Continuing his description of the Hebrew religion, Dr. Smith says, " It advanced no further than to the belief that its God was superior in power as well as in character to all other gods, and thus Lord of the whole earth." This statement is contradicted by the explicit declarations of the prophets, who, from the time of Isaiah onward, proclaim not only the nothingness of idols, but also the absoluteness of God.

[1] Chap. ix. 6.

The oldest Hebrew writers, though they regard Jehovah as a great moral Being, incomparably greater and stronger than any of the other gods, generally speak of him as "the God of Israel," and not as the only existing God; so that they seem not to have attained to the idea that there can be but one God. The belief that other nations had their gods was, apparently, accepted by them as a matter of course.

In contrast to this way of speaking, however, the canonical prophets declare emphatically that the gods of the heathen are "no gods, but the work of men's hands;"[1] "dumb idols," which cannot move, much less speak and help.[2] With an equal emphasis they declare, not simply that there is no god among the nations like Jehovah, but that there is no god anywhere except him. "Before me there was no God formed, neither shall there be after me," says Isaiah.[3] Again, he asks, "Is there a God beside me?" Answering his own question, he says, "I know not any."[4] In the same para-

---

[1] Isa. xxxvii. 19.   [2] Hab. ii. 18, 19.   [3] Chap. xliii. 10.   [4] Chap. xliv. 8.

graph he affirms the absoluteness of Israel's God.[1]

Regarding Jehovah as a living moral person, transcendent in holiness as well as in wisdom and power, the prophets were led to conceive that, as Jehovah alone was the Holy One, then, as the Holy One, he alone was God. Thus, as the result of their lofty ethical conception of his being, they were enabled to see that, if one such divine person exist, no other divine person can exist. Hence they represent him as the Lord of the whole earth, not because he is "superior in power as well as in character to all other gods," but because all other gods are nothing, and he is God alone.

To his other assertion that the Jew, hampered by lingering tribalism, was unable to "form a conception of the universality and majesty of the moral law such as we find in Plato or in Cicero," one need simply reply that Israel's specialty was not philosophy, but religion. Her representative writers were religious teachers, most of whom lived and wrote

[1] Isa. xliv. 6.

before the time when philosophical speculation began to take definite shape in the scientific systems of Plato and Aristotle. Hence we should not look in the Old Testament for abstract statements of reasoned truth, but for practical statements of moral and religious truth.

If, however, the Jew, who was nothing if not religious, could not form a conception of the moral law as high and broad as Plato and Cicero could, he did form a conception of the moral Law-giver as pure and exalted as they did; and, if his statements of moral truth were not as scientific as theirs, his ideas of moral duty were as adequate. No nation other than the Jews entertained such a lofty conception of the Deity as a transcendent moral person; and no religion other than Judaism laid such emphasis on justice between man and man, on mercy to both man and beast, or on meekness and humility before God.

A tree is known and should be tested by its fruit. The moral teaching of both Greece and Rome was, doubtless, influenced more or less by

Judaism; but, whether it was influenced much or little by the Jews, if the moral conceptions of the former nations were so superior to those of the latter nation, why did the Greeks and Romans not do more for the ethical advancement, or the moral elevation, of mankind? Was it not because in them the deep moral sense and the pure religious spirit, which belonged preeminently to the Jews, were largely wanting?

And how did it come to pass that Judaism was the only ancient religion capable of developing into a universal religion such as it became many centuries before it culminated in Christianity? Was it not that the idea of the unity of humanity, an idea which the progress of mankind has made more clear from age to age, originated in the Hebrew conception that all men have been created in the moral image of God, so that, since all are related to him as their Creator, they are also related to one another as his creatures?

Thus, whatever may have been his conception of the universality and majesty of the moral law, the influence of the Jew on moral life and character has been immeasurably greater than that of either the Greek or the Roman; for it is owing to the influence of the Jewish, and not the Grecian or the Roman, religion that the human race has, for upwards of two thousand years, been steadily advancing towards universal brotherhood.

CHAPTER XIII.

MORALITY.

OBJECTING to a weak as well as an unwise defence, by the editor of *Lux Mundi*, of the most startling of the so-called imprecatory Psalms, the essayist says, "This is the way in which we have been led by our traditional belief in the inspiration of the Old Testament to play fast and loose with our understandings and with our moral sense." He thus criticises the imperfect character of the Old Testament morality.

However much old-fashioned ideas of inspiration may have misled apologists in the past, the best expositors at present do not, in their interpretation of the revengeful imprecations of the Old Testament, play fast and loose either with understanding or with moral sense. On the contrary, they regard the dictates of the one as sacredly as they regard the sanctions of the other.

While they perceive that, in the majority of vindictive passages, the speaker or the psalmist, as the case may be, zealous for the honor of Jehovah, so identifies himself with God that he considers God's enemies his enemies, and hates them simply because, being evil, they are the enemies of good, they frankly admit with Dr. Moll, in Lange's "Biblework," that Psalm cix. displays a spirit "which is not free from carnal passion." It exhibits a vindictiveness, indeed, which even Hebrew ethics at its point of highest development condemns.

The true explanation of the revengeful spirit here displayed is found in the difference between the view-point of the Law and the view-point of the Gospel—a difference indicated by our Lord's rebuke to his disciples for manifesting the zeal of Elijah, when they desired him to imitate the spirit of the Old Testament dispensation by commanding fire from heaven to consume the inhabitants of a hostile village.[1]

[1] Luke ix. 51–56.

The Bible records a progressive morality. No one can carefully study it without perceiving a progress in moral teaching, as well as a development in religious doctrine; nor can any one impartially compare the Law of Moses with the Gospel of Christ without observing a difference of moral standard in them. Just as we can trace a progress, with the lapse of centuries, from a lower to a higher state of civilization among the Hebrew people, so we can trace a progress, under divine enlightenment, from a less perfect to a more perfect apprehension of moral and religious truth in their sacred Scriptures.

There is, in fact, a perceptible difference between the earlier and the later ideas on almost every subject. The more ancient writings present such views of truth as were obtainable by men who had reached a stage of partial religious development; the more modern writings present such views as could be obtained by men who had arrived at a stage of complete religious development. In these latter writings, we find not only higher standards of morality, but also clearer perceptions of duty and loftier ideals of life.

Owing to the incomplete development of spiritual ideas under the old dispensation, men's conceptions of morality were necessarily imperfect. Without miraculous inspiration, which the Scriptures do not warrant, much less claim, perfect conceptions of moral truth were then impossible. Hence the Old Testament characters could not reasonably have been expected to speak and act according to the exalted standard of the Sermon on the Mount.

But, it may be asked, is inspiration compatible with imperfect morality? Certainly, it is; because, if a man honestly conforms to the highest moral standard of his time, he is a truly moral man. By acting in conformity with the moral standard of his age, an inspired man would have the testimony of his conscience; and to a soul in fellowship with God this testimony is itself a means of clarifying the spiritual vision.

Inspiration impels a man to speak and act in harmony with all the light he has, and with all the knowledge he can get; but neither Moses nor Elijah was inspired to anticipate the ethical and spiritual statements of Christ. That inspiration is compatible with immorality no rational teacher maintains; but that inspiration is compatible with imperfect or crude morality may be consistently maintained, because, as Dr. A. B. Bruce says, "Crude morality is compatible with a good conscience."[1]

Such examples of cruelty and treachery, therefore, as the slaughter of the Canaanites, the killing of Sisera, the assassination of Eglon, the slaying of Agag by Samuel, the massacre of the prophets by Elijah, and the hanging of Haman with his ten sons, which Dr. Smith considers "responsible in no small degree for murderous persecutions, and for the extirpation or oppression of heathen races," were quite in keeping with the vindictive spirit, as well as with the crude morality, of Old Testament times.

It seems most unfair of him, however, to hold the Old Testament responsible for their deplo-

[1] *Contemporary Review*, July, 1894.

rable effect on fanatical minds, when those professing Christians who may have been influenced by them to oppress or persecute others possessed the positive precepts of the perfect Christ, and were guilty of great inconsistency in failing to manifest his mild and merciful spirit.

Deeds of violence, like those just enumerated, could, doubtless, have been justified by the persons who committed them, in harmony with the highest moral standards which then existed; but a wise apologist does not think of defending such deeds any more than he would undertake to defend the treachery of Jael, the duplicity of Rahab, the deception of Jacob, or the adultery of David.

He simply claims that we should judge such incidents, not according to the complete statements of Christian ethics, but according to the crude conceptions of the age in which they occurred, always bearing in mind that the ethical ideas of the Old Testament are parts of a gradually unfolding system of morality which culminated in the perfect teaching of the New Testament Christ.

CHAPTER XIV.

BARBARITY.

COMMENTING on the cruelties connected with the settlement of Palestine, and complaining of the inconsistent replies which foolish apologists have made to the objections raised by humanity against the slaughter of the Canaanites, the essayist says, "We are in no way bound to believe that God so identified himself with a favored tribe as to license it to invade a number of other tribes which had done it no wrong, to slaughter them and take possession of their land." He thus criticises the inhuman character of the Old Testament barbarity.

True apologists do not attempt to justify the butcheries and barbarities of the ancient Hebrew wars, or to maintain that Israel had a legal right to the land of Canaan. They neither claim that, in conquering the country, the Israelites did but recover their own, nor hold that, having been driven by force from Egypt, they had a right to help themselves to a home where they could find it, by putting all the existing inhabitants to the sword; nor do they fall back upon the simple command of God, justifying it on the ground that the Canaanites were idol-worshippers and, consequently, ignorant of the true God.

They believe it to have been the purpose of Providence that the Israelites should possess Canaan, just as they believe it to have been his purpose that the Puritans should possess New England; but they do not consider Providence responsible for the inhumanities either of Israelites or of Puritans. Each people took its own way to secure possession of its providential inheritance.

Instead of holding that "God so identified himself with a favored tribe as to license it to invade a number of other tribes which had done it no wrong, to slaughter them and take possession of their land," modern apologists hold that the Hebrew leaders so identified themselves with Jehovah that they regarded anything done in his name as a divine design. Every prompting to do what they believed to be his will, or to accomplish what they believed to be his desire, was conceived and described by them as a divine suggestion, or a divine command. Jehovah told them or impelled them, they considered, so to act.

The explanation of this fact is very simple. The Israelites were not a philosophic, but a religious, people. Unaccustomed to philosophical speculation, but impressed with physical phenomena as manifestations of the Deity, they beheld God everywhere, and traced his agency in everything. They heard his voice in the thunder; they saw his hand in the lightning; they felt his frown in the cloud.

Connecting everything directly with God, the Old Testament writers did not duly discriminate between a natural consequence and a divine design. As Bishop Perowne says, " The Biblical writers drew no sharp, accurate line between events as the consequence of the divine order and events as following from the divine purpose.

To them all was ordained and designed of God."[1]

The Hebrew writers saw no place for chance or accident in creation, because, in their view of Providence, nothing was disconnected from divine causality. To them God was the immediate author of all phenomena in nature, as well as of all happenings in history and all occurrences in life. Believing that everything was of God, they likewise believed that everything was designed of him. As all events were in his hand and under his direction, they naturally supposed that evil as well as good proceeded from him.

Consistently with the view that even the movements of the mind were owing to his influence, they spoke of him as hardening man's heart, and also as tempting man to sin. Since, however, "God cannot be tempted with evil, and he himself tempteth no man,"[2] all those expressions which represent him as prompting men either to be cruel or to do evil should be interpreted as Hebrew forms of speech that originated in a Semitic mode of thought.

[1] Explanatory note on Ps. li. 4.   [2] James i. 13.

Thus the harsher features of the Old Testament are capable of a rational explanation, and, in this sense, of a sufficient vindication. In their conquest of Canaan, the Israelites adopted the methods of warfare that were characteristic of their age; and, impelled by a religious motive, they dealt with their captives in such a way as they believed would, in the circumstances, promote the purest worship of Jehovah and the highest welfare of his people.

If any one, however, perpetrated butcheries and barbarities which were not justifiable from a truly religious point of view, his acts were not simply condemned, but he himself was held to be guilty of blood. Hence the house of Jehu, many of whose murders and massacres were as unnecessary as they were atrocious, was doomed to have his blood-guiltiness avenged upon it.

For, although the writer of the second book of the Kings[1] commended some things that this cruel monarch did, such as the destruction of the house of Ahab, yet the prophet Hosea,[2] with a deep insight into the ways of Providence,

---

[1] Chap. x. 30. [2] Chap. i. 4.

declared that the blood of Jezreel should be visited upon the house of Jehu, because, not satisfied with executing vengeance on the guilty, Jehu had slaughtered the innocent as well.

CHAPTER XV.

SACRIFICE.

INDICATING the leading features of Hebrew law, he comes at length to the sacrificial worship of the Israelites; and, though he remarks the absence from the Mosaic ritual of human sacrifice, which was practised even by the polished Athenians, the essayist takes occasion to say that "all sacrifice is irrational." He thus criticises the irrational character of the Old Testament sacrifice.

Many of the heathen conceptions of sacrifice were, doubtless, irrational; but the sacrifices of the Old Testament present a marked contrast to those of pagan peoples. Among the heathen, sacrifices were regarded as a means of appeasing the divine anger, or of averting the divine vengeance; among the Hebrews, they were regarded as an evidence of dependence and an indication of indebtedness. In the one case, the offering was supposed to satisfy an imaginary want in God; in the other case, it was known to express a sensible need in man.

The first offerings mentioned in Scripture are thank-offerings, which were presented to Jehovah as symbols of gratitude and praise; and by the Old Testament writers sacrifices are viewed, not as gifts with which a man rendered the Deity propitious, or as payments by which he purchased the forgiveness of his sins, or as performances by which he fulfilled his obligations to Jehovah, but rather as symbolic expressions, not only of the penitent faith by which he sought reconciliation and communion with God, but also of the sincere devotion by which he proved his readiness to discharge the moral and spiritual duties that belong to life.

Even the propitiatory sacrifices of the Bible are but symbols of reconciliation and communion between man and God. Sensible of spiritual need, the human spirit desires fellowship with the Divine Spirit; and, conscious of moral transgression, the human conscience seeks relief from condemnation by giving practical proof of its repentance. Man has a sense of sin, as well as a sense of need. As a conscious sinner, he feels himself at variance with the Holy One whose laws he has broken and whose commands he has ignored; but, on laying his enmity aside, he is desirous of doing something that will restore him to the favor of the benignant Being who is willing to be reconciled to all men, and wants all men to be reconciled to him.

In an uncultivated and undeveloped state, man endeavors to establish a relation of reconciliation and communion between himself and his Maker by giving to the Deity a portion of what the Deity has given to him; in a more cultivated and developed state, man endeavors to establish this relation of harmony by consecrating himself and his substance to God. Hence, in principle, sacrifice is simply the putting of a part of oneself, so to speak, into that which one devotes to God; and such an act can scarcely be regarded as irrational.

Sacrifice, like worship, is an instinctive element in human nature. Its existence, in some form, ever since the earliest ages of mankind, and its practice, at some time, by all the greatest nations of antiquity, indicate that it is a spontaneous expression of reverence, repentance and devotion on the part of a finite being towards the Supreme Being, on whom he finds himself dependent, to whom he feels himself responsible, and with whom he wants to be at peace.

Made in the moral image of his Maker, man longs for fellowship with the Divine. This likeness, or relationship, constitutes the fundamental ground of sacrifice. "Man offers," says Oehler, "in virtue of his inalienable divine image, which makes it impossible for him to abstain from seeking that communion with God for which he was created, by such active self-devotion as takes place in offerings."[1]

In its devouter moods, at least, the human soul, because of its divine kinship, is drawn by a sort of natural impulse to express in deeds, as well as in words, its obligation of indebtedness to God. That inward prompting which impels a man to offer prayer or praise, impels him also

[1] "Theology of the Old Testament," Am. edition, p. 266.

to offer sacrifice of some kind, either outward or inward, or both. The same instinct that leads him to perform acts of devotion, leads him, according to his education and development, to perform acts of service or sacrifice. Thus, generally speaking, the essential nature of an offering is the devotion of man to God expressed in an outward act.

In contrast to the abominable practices connected with the sacrificial worship of the heathen, the Old Testament sacrifices express the deepest religious instincts of the human heart; but, not having risen to the conception that man should consecrate himself and his all to God, the Hebrew people, realizing that everything came from him, offered him a part of what they had received at his hand. Their offerings, being proofs of allegiance as well as tokens of love, evidenced a right disposition towards him.

The observance of the Mosaic ritual served not only to discipline the Israelites in purity and regularity of worship, but also to teach them the great truth that man should give something of himself to the object of his devotion. Hence the adoption and perpetuation of an ancient rite, that belonged to a primitive state of existence and an elementary stage of revelation, helped to develop a fundamental religious idea, which was purified and spiritualized, from age to age, till the conception culminated in the doctrine of heart-devotion to God and self-sacrifice for man.

CHAPTER XVI.

ELECTION.

REPRESENTING the Deity as having "entered into a covenant with the sheik's tribe," as he calls the descendants of Abraham, "to the exclusion of the rest of the human race," the essayist asks, "Can we imagine the Author of the universe limiting his providential regard and his communication of vital truth to his creatures by tribal lines?" He thus criticises the partial character of the Old Testament election.

We cannot, of course, imagine either arbitrariness or partiality in a perfect Being. Such a thing is inconceivable. Nor do the Scriptures furnish the slightest ground for such imagining. The supposition that the Bible anywhere suggests an idea so inconsistent with the righteous character of God, is based upon a misunderstanding, a very serious misunderstanding, of its teaching. Dr. Smith's own remarks, for example, contain no fewer than three popular misconceptions.

In the first place, according to the record in the book of Genesis, the covenant of Jehovah with Abraham was not made to the exclusion of any race, but rather to the inclusion of every race. "In thee," or, "in thy seed," the record reads, "shall all the families (nations) of the earth be blessed."[1] These words clearly teach that all men should in some manner derive blessing through Abraham and his posterity.

While the sacred writers represent God as having a covenant relation to the Israelites, they also represent him as having a covenant purpose concerning the world. The gracious divine purpose of revelation and redemption, which is expressed in so many Old Testament passages, though it has a primary reference to Israel, may be shown to have, in every case, an ultimate reference to mankind. There was thus no favoritism implied in the Abrahamic covenant.

[1] Gen. xii. 3; xxii. 18.

As set forth in Scripture, the election of the Israelites was simply a conditional choice of a certain people, on account of a special fitness for a certain work. Owing to these circumstances solely, God chose one race that through it, or by means of it, the blessings of his truth might come upon all races. There is, therefore, nothing arbitrary about the doctrine of divine election.

Election is not the outcome of an unconditional decree. It rests neither upon divine sovereignty nor upon human merit, but upon a particular attitude towards God and a peculiar fitness for his service. Qualification is the only ground of preference with God. He is an ethical Being, who has equal moral relations with all men; and, on the same principle on which he chose the Israelites, he chooses men to-day.

In the second place, instead of teaching that God limits the manifestation of his providential regard to his creatures by tribal lines, the Old Testament teaches a divine superintendence that extends to all men, so that they all are sharers alike in the care of Providence. The author of

Psalm lxv., for instance, represents God as the hearer of prayer, to whom all flesh may come, and likewise as "the confidence of all the ends of the earth."[1]

One more example of universal providence may be given. The book of Amos represents God as having granted the same providential guidance to the other nations that was granted to the Hebrews. Threatening his people with divine judgment on account of their transgressions, the Prophet of Tekoa tells them that, as Jehovah had led them out of Egypt, so also he had led the Philistines from Caphtor, and the Syrians from Kir.[2]

The idea that the Israelites were the special favorites of Heaven and the exclusive objects of divine care, is a foolish Pharisaic notion, which has no foundation whatsoever in the Bible. The providence of God, like the government of God, is as wide as the world, and is not restricted in its exercise, as Judaism, contrary to the doctrine of its own Scriptures, arrogantly and unreasonably assumed. The Old Testament distinctly

[1] Verses 2, 5.   [2] Chap. ix. 7, 8.

teaches that God is equally present in mercy, as well as in judgment, in the affairs of every nation on the earth.

In the third place, instead of teaching that God limits the communication of his vital truth to men by tribal lines, the ancient Scriptures teach that, while the heathen had some true knowledge of God, relatively it was not so large as that which Israel possessed. The belief that in ancient times the Jews were the sole depositaries of divine truth, is simply an ecclesiastical assumption. Other nations were in comparative, not in utter, darkness.

God is a self-manifesting Being, a knowledge of whom cannot be confined to the members of a single race. He is also an impartial Being, whose revelation, like whose love, is given to all men in proportion as they revere and serve him. The whole tenor of Old Testament teaching is that, so far as its relation to him will permit, God does as much, in his protecting providence and by his revealing spirit, for one nation as he does for another.

Thus, as there was nothing arbitrary in God's

election of the Israelites, so there was nothing partial in his treatment of them. They enjoyed no monopoly either of favor or of love. They were the recipients of special divine favor, and the objects of special divine regard, only so long as they were the subjects of special devotion to God.

CHAPTER XVII.

ANTHROPOMORPHISM.

ALLUDING to an event recorded in Genesis, which represents Jehovah as appearing to Abraham and as being entertained by the patriarch, the essayist asks, "Why should we force ourselves to believe that the Being who fills eternity and infinity became the guest of a Hebrew sheik?" He thus criticises the absurd character of the Old Testament anthropomorphism.

We do not force ourselves to believe anything so utterly contrary to reason. Dr. Smith asks this question as though modern scholars interpreted the anthropomorphic language of Scripture literally, whereas he knows that they regard all those expressions, which seem to ascribe to God the possession of bodily parts and organs, such as hands and feet, eyes and ears, mouth and nose, simply as symbolic.

The ascription to God in early times of parts and organs analogous to those of men was as natural as it was universal. In a state of partial development, mankind naturally form a mental image of the Divine Being after the likeness of a human being. "Only in the fancy of a God made in the image of man," as Miss Wedgwood has aptly said, "can the infant race approach the truth that man is formed in the image of God."[1] With young or undeveloped persons such a fancy is as common to-day as it was in the days of the patriarchs.

The symbolic application to God, moreover, of terms which properly relate to men, is as reasonable as it is natural. In accordance with our mental constitution, divine truths can be neither conceived by us nor conveyed to us without the employment of such figurative language; and, since the bulk of mankind can approximate to a notion of the Absolute One only by means of figured conceptions, the use of anthropomorphic symbols is the only possible way in which the Infinite Being can be made intelligible to the finite mind.

[1] "The Message of Israel," p. 82.

But, while the Hebrew Scriptures represent God as walking and talking, hearing and seeing, remembering and forgetting, resolving and repenting, and the like, they distinctly teach that he is a spiritual Being who cannot be seen, as well as an infinite and eternal Being who does not change; so that there is nothing perplexing, much less preposterous, about their use of anthropomorphic expressions and representations.

When the essayist, therefore, asks, "Why should we force ourselves to believe that the Being who fills eternity and infinity became the guest of a Hebrew sheik?" he is well aware, not only that the Old Testament teaches the spirituality and unchangeableness of God, but also that the eighteenth chapter of Genesis, to which he here refers, contains an account belonging to a time when it was generally believed that men sometimes entertained angels and even gods, and that, consequently, the account is to be explained as an anthropomorphic representation of an ancient manifestation of the divine presence.

The compilers of the Pentateuch leave no

doubt in the minds of their readers as to how such a representation should be understood. They elsewhere show that its language is not to be taken literally. In harmony with the Apostle's declaration that "no man hath seen God at any time,"[1] they report Moses as saying, by inspiration, of Jehovah, "Thou canst not see my face; for man shall not see me and live."[2]

This representation, therefore, like all other representations of a similar kind, must be interpreted in accordance with the primitive form of the account and the symbolic character of its language. Hence we are not to infer from the description that the Deity really exists in the shape of a man, or that he actually appeared to Abraham with a human body, and walked and talked and ate with the old patriarch!

In the sphere of representative thought, no religion can dispense entirely with anthropomorphic expressions. If we conceive of things spiritual at all, we are compelled to form our conceptions of them in terms borrowed from things material; and, as we cannot find words

---

[1] John i. 18. [2] Exod. xxxiii. 20.

in which to express our conceptions of the Deity, or to record his manifestations of himself, except by analogies derived from things cognizable by our senses, the language of revelation, like the language of adoration, must be anthropomorphic and symbolic.

Anthropomorphism is just as peculiar to New Testament as it was to Old Testament times. In some form and to some extent, it belongs to the religious phraseology of all times. Our conceptions of the Deity are more adequate than were those of the patriarchs, and, as a consequence, our representations of him are more refined than theirs were; but so long as we worship him as a person (and we cannot rationally worship anything but a person), we must make use of anthropomorphic expressions. There is no possible escape from using them. To abolish anthropomorphism is to abolish theism.

Primitive anthropomorphism was uncritical, Jewish anthropomorphism was unphilosophical; but Christian anthropomorphism is both critical and philosophical. Those, therefore, who regard the Divine Being as a personal spirit, having moral relations with the world, a spirit that is infinitely more a person than is any one of us, need never fear the use of anthropomorphic terms, or dread the criticism of them by antichristian men.

CHAPTER XVIII.

MIRACLE.

MAKING frequent strange references to the miraculous events recorded in the earlier books of the Bible, such as the destruction of the cities of the Plain and the turning of Lot's wife into a pillar of salt, the essayist singles out "the strange episode of Balaam and his colloquy with his ass," and comments on "the stopping of the sun and moon that Israel might have time for the pursuit and slaughter of his enemies." He thus criticises the inadequate character of the Old Testament idea of miracle.

One peculiarity of the Old Testament is that, during the period of the patriarchs, it contains no reference to a miracle, in the technical sense of the term. That is to say, in the patriarchal age, it makes no mention of a miracle wrought by man as the credential of a commission received from God; so that, in primeval times, a miracle seems to have been regarded, not as a special attestation of a divinely commissioned teacher, but as a marvellous display of divinely exerted power, or of divinely manifested wisdom and grace.

The first person mentioned in Scripture who is said to have been endowed with the gift of performing miracles is Moses; and, as the miracles ascribed to him are of the nature of special providences, due to the operation of natural laws under the superintendence of God, they have been denominated providential miracles. Such miracles as the Twelve Plagues are practically synonymous with divine interventions, or providential interpositions.

The account of the destruction of the cities of the Plain[1] is a graphic description of an ancient volcanic eruption, a kind of catastrophe to which the valley of the Lower Jordan, from its geological structure, is said by Christian scientists to have been subject at one time. The sudden overthrow of Sodom and the neighboring cities

[1] Gen. xix. 23-29.

by some sort of inflammable substance, such as bitumen, was thus due to natural causes, as Sir William Dawson has clearly shown.[1] The subsequent turning of Lot's wife into a pillar of salt was likewise due to natural causes, as he has also shown, her body having become incrusted with liquid lava in the form of saline mud, which usually accompanies a bitumen eruption.

Such physical phenomena would now be called extraordinary rather than miraculous; but by the people of an unscientific age they were considered marvellous displays of supernatural power. Each of these uncommon and exceptional occurrences was rendered miraculous to the mind of the narrator by its association with a special manifestation of divine justice, the former being regarded as a just condemnation of sin, the latter being regarded as a just punishment for disobedience.

The story of Balaam[2] is a traditional account of an ancient angelic appearance, belonging to a time when the idea of animals talking with

[1] *Expositor*, January, 1886.   [2] Num. xxii. 22-35.

men was practically universal, and is to be interpreted in accordance with that fact. The account of the sun and moon standing still[1] also belongs to a time when men had no strictly scientific conception either of the nature of a miracle or of the constitution of the universe; so that, consistently with its true character, the best modern expositors regard the phenomenon it describes as a prolongation of the daylight by the ordinary laws of atmospheric refraction.

The parenthetic passage which contains the account of this extraordinary phenomenon is cited from the book of Jasher, a well-known collection of national songs, and gives a poetic description of a remarkable victory gained by Joshua over the Amorites through the intervention of natural means. Being part of an ancient poem, the citation must be interpreted as Oriental poetry.

The explanation of the passage given in the "Critical Commentary" is worth reproducing here. "The language of a poem is not to be literally interpreted, and, therefore, when the sun

[1] Josh. x. 12-15.

and moon are personified, addressed as intelligent beings, and represented as standing still, the explanation is, that the light of the sun and moon was supernaturally prolonged by the same laws of refraction and reflection that ordinarily cause the sun to appear above the horizon, when he is in reality below it."

According to the derivation of the term, a miracle is a wonder-causing event. Such an event is designated by the Hebrew writers in a twofold way. Viewing it from its negative side, they designate it by a word which signifies an object of wonder; viewing it from its positive side, they designate it by a word which signifies an act of power. In the former aspect, a miracle means an extraordinary occurrence of some sort; in the latter aspect, it means a supernatural manifestation of some kind.

All the marvellous events recorded in the Old Testament come under the one or the other of these two classes of miracle; and, before attempting to explain such an event, we must first ascertain the class to which it belongs. Having determined its character, we must then interpret the passage in which it occurs in accordance with Semitic modes of thought, as well as in accordance with figurative and anthropomorphic forms of expression, always remembering that a miracle is not a suspension, much less a violation, of the laws of the universe, but something wonderful that has happened in the providence of God, or something remarkable that has been performed by the power of God, in harmony with nature's laws.

CHAPTER XIX.

PROPHECY.

SPEAKING of the prophetic element in them, the essayist says, "No real and specific prediction of the advent of Jesus, or of any event in his life, can be produced from the books of the Old Testament." He thus criticises the indefinite character of the Old Testament prophecy of Christ.

This statement is incomplete and its implication is untrue. It implies that the Old Testament contains no prophecies of a future Messiah which were properly fulfilled in the New Testament Christ, whereas, from the time of Isaiah, the son of Amoz, the canonical prophets put forth the conception of an ideal Coming One, who as a divinely anointed King should reign over the Israelites as the perfected people of God.

An explicit reference to the advent of this God-appointed King occurs in the ninth chapter of the book of Isaiah,[1] where the prophet announces the birth of a child who should sit as a Prince of Peace upon the throne of David, to establish the theocratic kingdom, and to uphold it with justice and righteousness. Such was to be the character of the ideal person who was expected in the future.

Nothing is here said of the time when the promised prince should appear and publicly manifest himself as the peaceful ruler of God's people, so that in one sense prophecy is indefinite; but from this period the prophetic ministry fostered in the minds of the Israelites the hope of a future Messiah, and unfolded to the faith of the Israelites the fundamental principles of the spiritual kingdom which he was to establish on the earth.

The Old Testament references to this exalted personage are of a general or, better, an official nature, because, during the period of the canonical prophets, the conception of the Messiah had

[1] Verses 6, 7.

not reached its full development; and, as each prophet published his description of the Coming One in harmony with the stage to which the conception had developed in his own day, the prophetic representations are expressed rather in temporal than in spiritual forms. So long, however, as Hebrew prophecy continued, the hope of a future Messiah became more bright, and the perception of his character more clear, as time went on.

But, while the Coming One was perceived by the prophets only in the great outlines of his character and office and work, still he was represented by them as a ruler,[1] a counsellor,[2] a teacher, and a deliverer or saviour,[4] all of which representations were spiritually fulfilled in Jesus of Nazareth; for, when the fulness of time came, he as God's Messiah appeared on the earth, and bore the character and exercised the office and performed the work which the ancient Scriptures shadowed forth.

[1] Isa. ix. 2-7; Jer. xxiii. 5, 6; xxxiii. 15; Micah v. 2-5.
[2] Isa. xi. 1-10. [3] Ezek. xxxiv. 23, 24; xxxvii. 24, 25.
[4] Zech. ix. 9.

Hence the Evangelists were not "simple-minded," as Dr. Smith says, but sensible-minded, when they found "in the sacred books of their nation prognostications of the character and mission of Jesus," inasmuch as such prognostications or foreshadowings of him really occur in them. What the prophecies foreshadowed the Son of Man fulfilled.

The view of prophecy presented "by modern divines such as Keith," is uncritical, of course. His work on prophecy was written from the standpoint of traditionalism, as Dr. Smith well knows, and was published before the scientific study of the Bible had fairly commenced. His view assumes that a prophet was a predictor who possessed "the most perfect knowledge of futurity,"[1] whereas a prophet was a man divinely influenced to communicate spiritual truth, whether he foretold future events or not. He was an inspired teacher whose office it was to declare the divine will and to interpret the divine purpose, whether his declarations and interpretations related to the past, to the present, or to the future.

[1] "Keith on Prophecy," abridged edition, p. 18.

Prophecy was not something magical or mechanical performed by superhuman beings, who possessed miraculous foresight, but something moral and religious proclaimed by spiritual-minded men, who acted under supernatural influence. Though it gradually unfolded God's purpose of redemption for the world through his Messiah, yet it was not the miraculous prediction of future events, but the inspired utterance of divine truth. Like apostolic preaching, prophetic teaching was moral and religious instruction imparted by the aid of the Holy Spirit.

The essayist makes another unfortunate misstatement, however, when he says respecting the prophetic utterances of the Old Testament, that "at most we find passages or phrases which are capable of a spiritual application (to Jesus), and in that metaphorical sense prophetic." The spiritual teaching of the Old Testament is prophetic, irrespective of its application in the New Testament to Christ; and all the personal Messianic prophecies, such as those indicated at the bottom of a preceding page,[1] not only refer

---
[1] Page 133.

officially to Jesus, but also find their true fulfilment in him.

Though we should not assert the complete identity of Old Testament prophecy with New Testament fulfilment, because the prophetic representations of the Messiah were partly temporal and partly spiritual, owing to the partial development of the conception of the Messiah in pre-christian times, nevertheless, we may and should assert that spiritually and officially Messianic prophecy, so far as it was capable of a literal fulfilment, was solely and exclusively fulfilled in him whom God hath anointed to be not simply a Prince of Peace, but the Saviour of the world.

CHAPTER XX.

IMMORTALITY.

Discussing the doctrine of a future life, the essayist says, "Of a belief in the immortality of the soul no evidence can be found in the Old Testament, though readers of the Bible who persist in using the unrevised version may remain under the impression that the doctrine is found in Job." He thus criticises the undeveloped character of the Old Testament conception of immortality.

This assertion is both ambiguous and incorrect. The assertion is ambiguous, because, in its developed form, the immortality of the soul is a New Testament doctrine. It was Christ, the apostle Paul declares, who "brought life and incorruption to light through the Gospel."[1] That is to say, it was Jesus who, by

[1] 2 Tim. i. 10.

means of the Gospel, threw light upon, or brought into greater clearness, the idea of an after-life, an idea which originated many centuries before he came.

The assertion is incorrect, because, while its idea of immortality is dim and indistinct, and while its teaching on the subject is fragmentary and indefinite, some evidence is found in the Old Testament of a belief in a future state of being. The vagueness or indefiniteness of its teaching in respect to immortality is owing partly to the undeveloped character of its conception, and partly to the unphilosophical character of its language. The Hebrew way both of thinking and speaking about immortality is quite different from ours.

Unlike the New Testament, the Old Testament does not contain a direct or formal statement in regard to immortality. The doctrine is nowhere precisely stated in the Hebrew books, because, in the minds of the writers, belief in a future life had not yet assumed the definite form of a doctrine. This belief did not rest on a distinct promise, but on a cherished conviction; and it is not expressed in positive or explicit utterances, but in hints and intimations which clearly imply continued existence for man after his life on earth has closed.

Unlike the Christian Scriptures, too, the Hebrew Scriptures do not partition man into body and soul, or into body and soul and spirit. They were written before such a distinction had been introduced by philosophy. Nor do they call that which survives of him at death either soul or spirit. In the Old Testament, as in the New, it is the immortality of the man, not the immortality of the soul, of which the sacred writers speak. An immortal soul, or a disembodied spirit, is not a scriptural, but a philosophical, expression.

The Hebrew Sheol, like the Greek Hades, represents, it is true, "a shadowy abode of the dead;" but, though conceived as a shadowy abode, the habitation of the dead was not conceived as a region of unconscious being. Neither the Hebrews nor the Greeks supposed that death was the end of personal existence, or that it involved the loss of personal identity.

Such a notion has no place in the literature of either nation. Without speaking definitely of a future life, each people taught that man existed after death in the form of a shade, which was independent of the body, and survived the crumbling of the latter into dust.

Though the Hebrews believed that man does not wholly cease to be when the body dies, but that his personality subsists in Sheol, or the underworld, they did not attempt to describe the mode of subsistence in the kingdom of the dead. So far, however, as can be gathered from the general teaching of their Scriptures, they thought of subsistence in Sheol as but a dim reflection of life on earth. Since existence here was supposed to be continued there in a dreamy, misty, shadowy form, they regarded the condition of men in the realm of the departed as the privation of all that belongs to life in the full sense of the term.

In the Old Testament, death is represented as a sort of sleep, out of which the shades of the departed in Sheol could be aroused into consciousness, as the prophecy of Isaiah plainly shows.[1] Referring to the entrance of the king of Babylon, not into the grave, but into Sheol,[2] the place of departed persons, the prophet graphically describes the commotion which his arrival might be supposed to make among the inhabitants of the unseen world. This description proves that the Old Testament teaches a belief in continued existence after death, as well as shows that, according to its teaching, the consciousness of deceased persons is not destroyed by death.

The continued existence of man after the body dies is a conception that goes right through the Old Testament, being found in the earlier no less than in the later books, except that the idea of immortality is somewhat more developed in the latter than in the former. To speak with Oehler, "Man's existence after death is treated in the Old Testament so much as a matter of course that the reality of it is never the subject of doubt."[3] It was not the reality, but the nature, of an after-existence that was called in

[1] Chap. xiv. 9-11. [2] Margin of Revised Version.
[3] "Theology of the Old Testament," Am. edition, p. 172.

question by the ancient Israelites. *That* the personality subsisted they believed; *how* it subsisted they could not tell.

In the Pentateuchal books, no reference is made to a future state; but belief in such a state is shown by the account of the taking of Enoch to God,[1] by the use of the word "Sheol"[2] with a sense that is quite distinct from the grave, and also by the occurrence of the expression, "gathered to his people,"[3] a formula that is not equivalent to the family sepulchre, and hence is not applicable to the final resting-place of the body.

In the historical books, nothing is said of a state of conscious being after death; but the account of the taking of Elijah to heaven,[4] as well as that of the raising of an apparition by the witch of Endor,[5] indicates belief in an afterexistence of some kind; and the language ascribed to David on the death of his young child implies belief in an after-existence with con-

---

[1] Gen. v. 24.   [2] Gen. xxxvii. 35.
[3] Gen. xxv. 8, 17; xxxv. 29; xlix. 33; Num. xx. 24.
[4] 2 Kings ii. 11.   [5] 1 Sam. xxviii. 14.

sciousness, otherwise the king would not have found comfort in the thought of meeting his child beyond the grave.[1]

In the prophetical books, the subsistence of all deceased persons, reduced to the condition of shades, but still retaining consciousness, is definitely expressed as a popular belief which the people of Israel, irrespective of their piety or their impiety, appear to have shared. The description of Sheol given by Isaiah,[2] and the picture of the same abode presented by Ezekiel,[3] furnish illustrations of the character of the conception in the days of the canonical prophets.

In the poetical books, belief in the personal continuance of man after death assumes the form of an assured conviction, or a definite faith. The book of Job,[4] whether one uses the revised or the unrevised version, contains the germ of a belief in a future state of fellowship with God, though the conception seems not to be so fully developed as it is in some of the Psalms. At all events, while the idea of an indissoluble union

[1] 2 Sam. xii. 23.   [2] Chap. xiv. 9-11.   [3] Chap. xxxii. 17-32.
[4] Chap. xiv. 13-15; xix. 23-27.

between the believing soul and the Supreme Being is evidently presupposed by the author of Job, it is more explicitly, if not more positively, expressed by certain of the psalmists.

By the Hebrew psalmists, right relation to God, or spiritual oneness with God, is regarded as a pledge of immortality. Because of this relation, one of them expresses the hope of a perpetual participation in joyous communion with God.[1] In consequence of such communion, another avows his faith in a satisfying vision of God which is to be perfectly realized by him at some period in the future.[2] Owing to a fellowship in righteousness between him and God, another utters an anticipation of escape from Sheol, which implies a belief that death is not for him the end of divine communion.[3] Realizing that God's presence makes man's blessedness both in heaven and on earth, another protests his expectation of eventually partaking of the glory of God;[4] and, finding his chief good in fellowship with God, he likewise declares his

---

[1] Ps. xvi. 11.   [2] Ps. xvii. 15.   [3] Ps. xlix. 15.
[4] Ps. lxxiii. 24.

confidence in a union with the Deity which can never be dissolved.[1]

Thus the Old Testament reveals evidence not only of a belief in immortality, but also of a development in the idea of immortality. There is a manifest progress from dimness to distinctness, from supposition to assurance, from belief to faith. The idea, presented in the earlier books vaguely and obscurely, is clearly and explicitly presented in the later books. Beginning with the belief that the relation into which God enters with the righteous, or the relation into which the righteous enter with him, will not be cancelled by death, it develops into the faith that a full and eternal fruition of the Divine Presence will be vouchsafed to all good people after death.

No distinction is drawn in the Hebrew Scriptures between the condition of the righteous and the condition of the wicked in the other world; but a difference in the relation of men to God here presupposes a difference in their relation to him hereafter.

[1] Ps. lxxiii. 26.

Among the Hebrews, belief in a future life did not so definitely assume the form of a doctrine as it did among the Egyptians. Notwithstanding its want of definiteness, however, the Old Testament presents a purer conception of immortality than is to be found in any other ancient literature. In the Hebrew Scriptures, there is not a trace of the old heathen idea that the body must be buried before the shade of the departed could find rest, or of the old Egyptian notion that the body had to be embalmed as a condition of the continued life of the soul. According to the Old Testament, it is the self, or the person, that survives at death; and the survival of the self is not supposed to be dependent on the preservation of the tabernacle in which the person dwells.

Though its statements respecting an after-life are not so clearly expressed as are those of the New, the Old Testament has a view of immortality that is distinctively its own; and, though its conception of immortality is not so fully developed as is that of the New, the Old Testament gives expression to all the main ideas of the Gospel in regard to a future state. Its teaching on the subject starts from the same premise, that life consists in fellowship with God; it proceeds upon the same assumption, that divine fellowship produces divine likeness; it leads to the same conclusion, that likeness to God is eternal and imperishable.

In the Old Testament, as in the New, life (life devoted to God, of course) is regarded not simply as the greatest earthly good, but as the only lasting good. In the Old as in the New Testament, too, immortality is considered rather a result than a reward of righteousness. He who makes God his portion has fellowship in righteousness with God; he who has such fellowship has living knowledge of the Divine; he who has this living knowledge is one with the Eternal, and he whose life is thus united to the Eternal has eternal life.

CHAPTER XXI.

QUALITIES.

THE admissions of the essayist deserve a brief consideration. While they are few in number compared with what the subject merits, most of them are significant; and, while some of them are made in rather qualified language, they are well worth summarizing.

Notwithstanding its faults and imperfections, Dr. Smith does not allege that "the Hebrew literature lacks qualities." On the contrary, though he finds some defects which do not fairly exist, and misses many excellences which are as conspicuous as they are important—such as its merciful provisions for animals, its wise regulations for cleanliness, its high standard of conjugal fidelity, its rigid regard for social and personal purity, its lofty moral teaching, and its transcendent spiritual wisdom—yet he admits that "the beauty, spiritual as well as lyrical," of certain parts of this literature is "beyond contest and almost beyond compare."

In the few pages devoted to the qualities of the Old Testament, he acknowledges "the magnificence of some parts of the prophetic writings;" he admires "both the religious exaltation and the lyrical excellence of some of the Psalms;" he appreciates "the beauty of the story of Joseph, and the book of Ruth;" he recognizes the dignity and unity which the Hebrew histories derive "from the continuous purpose which runs through them;" he asserts that Hebrew law "is an improvement in primitive law," and that "its Sabbath was most beneficent;" he admits that it "is comparatively hospitable and liberal in its treatment of the stranger," that its way of dealing with slaves "is more merciful than that either of Greece or Rome," that it "makes human life sacred," that it "forbids hereditary blood-feuds," that it "recognizes asylum" for the involuntary "homicide," and that it "mitigates the customs of war;" he allows that, "we shall hardly find anywhere a moral force equal in intensity to that of the Hebrew prophets;" he even allows that there is scarcely anything in Greek or Roman literature like the most notable passages "in the prophetic writings and the Psalms," which rebuke "the selfishness of wealth and the oppression of the poor."

With such a number of excellences, the Old Testament, regarded simply as a body of literature, has great intrinsic worth; but it also has merits of another kind. In addition to its literary and religious qualities, it has historical and doctrinal qualities which give it a peculiar value—a value that is not lessened in the least by any deficiency or inadequacy that is owing to imperfect ideas or undeveloped conceptions.

Historically, the Old Testament was a preparation for the New. Without the one we could not have had the other. Christianity is the historical continuation of Judaism, the one being the promise of which the other is the fulfilment. Christianity is thus rooted, so to speak, in the soil of Judaism. In consequence of this connection, the origin and evolution of

Christianity must be traced through Judaism; and, apart from the latter, the former can be neither explained nor understood.

Doctrinally, too, the Old Testament was and is an introduction to the New. Every vital truth in the one is germinally existent in the other. The divine element in the Law and the Prophets was the spiritual germ from which the Gospel evolved, the rudimental teaching out of which the doctrine of Christ was developed. In their inner spiritual contents, the Jewish Scriptures are an organic part of the Christian Scriptures. Because of this genetic relation, the Old Testament will always have a value similar to that of the New, and second only to that of the New.

The more the Old Testament books are studied as a body of Hebrew literature, the more clearly their true nature and their relative importance will be perceived; the more this literature is regarded as a record of divine revelation, the more highly both its history and its religion will be appreciated; the more the principles of the Law are compared with the principles of the

Gospel, the more fully it will be recognized that, in their fundamental doctrines, they are parts of one progressive manifestation of God; the more the organic connection between the Law and the Gospel is considered, the more generally it will be acknowledged that the revelation contained in the Old Testament was preparatory and introductory to that contained in the New, and that the revelation contained in the New Testament is not only the historical continuation, but also the doctrinal consummation, of that contained in the Old.

As the record of a series of partial revelations which prepared for, and culminated in, the perfect revelation of Christ, the Old Testament is related to the New as the root to the bud, the bud to the flower, or the flower to the fruit; so that, while the disuse of the Old would not affect the value of the New, it would affect our understanding of its doctrinal as well as its historical development. For this reason, the Old Testament has been, and is, and always will be, not a burden or a barrier, but a benefit and a blessing, to Christianity.

Such are, in brief, the qualities of the Old Testament. Hence it is not something which we should treat with neglect or indifference, but something which we should regard with interest and appreciation. Instead of being a weight for the Church to cast off, it is a treasure for the Church to store up; or, to change the figure, instead of being Christianity's millstone, it is rather Christianity's foundation-stone, because it forms the spiritual groundwork from which the·Christian superstructure rises, or on which the Christian system rests.

www.ingramcontent.com/pod-product-compliance
Lightning Source LLC
Chambersburg PA
CBHW030335170426
43202CB00010B/1132